Music Theory Essentials

A Step-by-Step Introduction to Music Theory for All Musicians

By: Barton Press

Copyright © 2020 by Barton Press

ALL RIGHTS RESERVED

No part of this book may be reproduced, stored in a retrieval system, or transmitted in any form or by any means, electronic, mechanical, photocopying, recording, scanning, or otherwise, without the prior written permission of the publisher.

Limit of Liability/Disclaimer of Warranty: the publisher and the author make no representations or warranties with respect to the accuracy or completeness of the contents of this work and specifically disclaim all warranties, including without limitation warranties of fitness for a particular purpose. No warranty may be created or extended by sales or promotional materials. The advice and strategies contained herein may not be suitable for every situation. This work is sold with the understanding that the publisher is not engaged in rendering medical, legal or other professional advice or services. If professional assistance is required, the services of a competent professional person should be sought. Neither the publisher nor the author shall be liable for damages arising herefrom. The fact that an individual, organization or website is referred to in this work as a citation and/or potential source of further information does not mean that the author or the publisher endorses the information the individuals, organization or website may provide or recommendations they/it may make. Further, readers should be aware that websites listed on this work may have changed or disappeared between when this work was written and when it is read.

Contents

Chapter 1: Introduction 1

Chapter 2: The Physics of Sound 6

Chapter 3: Basic Music Notation 18

Chapter 4: Intervals 30

Chapter 5: Scales 46

Chapter 6: Keys 62

Chapter 7: Music and Time 76

Chapter 8: Harmony and Chords 96

Chapter 9: Melody and Dynamics 110

Chapter 10: Final Thoughts 124

Chapter 1: Introduction

"Without music, life would be a mistake."
— *Friedrich Nietzsche, Twilight of the Idols*

Music theory is a sub-field of study under the more general subject area of musicology. The word musicology comes from the Greek words 'μουσική' (mousikē) for 'music' and 'λογος' (logos) for 'domain of study'), and so refers to the scholarly study of music. This includes examination of many diverse topics related to music, including the history of music, how music is understood and created in different cultures, and more recently, how music might be used therapeutically. However, while we might briefly touch on each of these three topics, the primary focus of this book will be on music theory.

Music theory is the study of what music is, how it is done, how it is organized, and how and why it can have such an effect on us.

First and foremost, music is created through sounds and silences. However, that is not all it is, nor is it just plain noise. Music is sounds or silences that are organized (whether by humans or machines) into carefully designed structures, patterns, or sequences, and with a variety of characteristics (e.g., pitch, duration, timbre) that are manipulated, with the goal of achieving some purpose.

And by how it is done, I mean not only the basics of how it is done or created (e.g., notes, scales, rhythms, etc.) but also what distinguishes those who do it well from those who do not, and what distinguishes those who do it well from each other.

Finally, as we all know from our own personal experiences, music can certainly create emotional reactions in us as listeners that go beyond other forms of communication. It may remind us of a sad experience in our life and perhaps even bring us to tears, or it may allow us to recapture the joy of a particularly happy moment and lift our spirits for the rest of the day. Something in music can move you—it can make you cry, remind you of a lost loved one, or bring you back to the happier days of your childhood.

Music may even have a physical effect on us. For example, it can cause us to experience a type of physical reaction known as a frisson (French, for "shiver"), also sometimes called a "tone chill". A frisson is an unexpected but pleasurable psychophysiological response to a particular auditory stimulus. Usually lasting only a few seconds, it is typically manifested as a "skin tingling" or "shiver up the spine" accompanied by "goosebumps," "hair standing on end," or pupil dilation.
Maybe it is the particular combination of sounds, or how they are organized, the silences between them, an unexpected change in the volume or key, or some other violation of musical expectations, that effects us in such a profound way. This is one of the questions that music theorists try to answer.

Music as Language

Music is often compared to language, and that comparison is a valid one. A language is also sounds (and silences) organized into carefully designed structures, sequences, or patterns, for the purpose of communicating ideas. The structures, sequences, and patterns that are more commonly used, form the grammar of that language, and the grammar then serves as guidelines for others to learn and use that language. However, the use of language is not and never should be limited by "grammatical rules" that require that it only be used as it has been used before. There should always be room for creativity. In fact, linguists recognize an entire area of study that focuses on the "pragmatics" of language, in other words, language as it is actually used by speakers, which is often inconsistent with the so-called "rules" of grammar. Grammatical rules are broken by all of us every day when we use slang, engage in everyday conversation, or when we send text messages to friends.

Actually, music may be thought of as a language used for communicating emotions. And while music theorists devote a lot of time to researching the how and why of compositions from musicians throughout history, in order to better understand how music has been done, they also recognize that these patterns should not be thought of as "rules" constraining the works of future composers. Even more so with music, creativity should not be constrained by what has been done before. Some have argued that not only is learning music theory a waste of time for musicians, it can actually negatively impact their efforts, because it teaches them to follow "rules", thus limiting and stifling their creativity. However, this would only be true if a musician blindly adhered to rules and conventions based on what was done in the past. But that is not what music theorists espouse, and even if they did, most musicians would never limit themselves in such a way anyhow. In the same way that a writer must learn to use language according to certain rules, but also know when to break those rules for the sake of achieving their objective or for the sake of creativity, being an effective composer of music requires finding the right balance between following the "rules" and breaking them. And breaking the rules will be much more meaningful if we know and understand what "rules" we are breaking and why. Just like any artist, the best composers know when and how to push the boundaries of their art and when not to.

Why Learn Music Theory?

Musicians, such as pianists, guitarists, drummers, oboe players, or vocalists, study music theory to understand what various instruments (or voices) are capable of doing and not doing, to learn and memorize pieces of music faster, and to be able to improvise more easily and effectively.

Composers study music theory to fully understand their compositional options, to understand how to create certain structures and produce certain effects in their own works, to create more complete and aesthetically pleasing compositions or music that elicits a desired emotional reaction, and to develop their own personal style.

Lyricists study music theory to produce songs that are maximally adapted for the specific characteristics of a particular performer's voice, or to produce music that sounds rich and creative, even when the accompaniment is simplified.

Music critics study music theory so they can fully appreciate and more carefully and effectively compare and evaluate the music of others.

Music educators study music theory so they can better understand a composer's intent for a given piece of music, and then explain that intent to their students, to enhance the student's performance.

Music therapists study music theory to better anticipate and even produce specific emotional effects on their clients, either by playing their own music, organizing performances by other musicians, or leading groups in music related activities.

The important concepts, vocabulary, and themes of music theory also allow us to speak with musicians and non-musicians in a common language. It serves as a shorthand for referring to important characteristics of the music. For example, if a piece of music in written in a specific musical "key" (a selected palette of notes), discussing or evaluating that music will be more effective if all involved in the discussion actually understand the concept of musical keys, how they function, and how they differ from one another.

Who Is This Book For?

This book is written for potential musicians who are just starting to learn to play an instrument, or for others like professional musicians, composers, lyricists, music critics, music educators, or music therapists, who understand the value of having a basic understanding of music theory. It should also be a good place to start for those who have had some musical experience or training in the past (e.g. participation in a choir, music lessons started but never finished, etc.) and who are now ready to delve into music a bit more thoroughly or in a much more committed way. This book should help you rediscover the joy of making music.

The concepts of music theory on which we will focus will be those of the European musical tradition, from the time of ancient Greece through the beginning of the 20th century.

What This Book Will Not Do

This book will not teach you to play music or play a particular instrument. It will, however, give you a basic understanding of music which can become a foundation for you to learn to play music, and it will discuss to some extent how playing music may differ between different types of instruments. But learning to play a particular instrument is a subject suitable for a separate book on just that one topic. Finally, this book will not teach you everything there is to know about music. An entire lifetime might be required for you to achieve that rather ambitious goal.

Chapter 2: The Physics of Sound

"If I were not a physicist, I would probably be a musician. I often think in music. I live my daydreams in music. I see my life in terms of music."
— *Albert Einstein*

Music is organized sound and silence. But what exactly is sound? Physicists understand that sound is created when mechanical pressure waves move through some physical medium, like air or water.

A "wave" can be roughly defined as a disturbance in something that otherwise would be calm (e.g., the surface of a body of water). Waves are seldom isolated disturbances, but instead form a repetitive and periodic pattern amounting to a series of waves moving in a direction away from whatever caused them. For example, multiple waves caused by dropping a rock into a tank of water will move (radiate) outwardly in a circle away from the point at which the rock entered the water. This type of wave is also known as a transverse wave because, as the movement away from the source occurs, there is also a corresponding up-and-down motion on the surface of the water at a right angle to the direction the wave is moving. You can experience this as you sit in a boat on a body of water. As the waves pass you, you feel yourself repeatedly lifted, up and down. Moreover, the height of the up and down movement of the waves is dependent largely on the intensity of the disturbance that caused them. In other words, the bigger the rock you drop into the water, the higher (or deeper) the up and down movement of the waves you create.

Figure 2.1: A Transverse Wave

However, the tiny pressure waves that create sound are not transverse waves but are longitudinal waves. A sound wave does not create a "bouncing up and down" movement like on the surface of water. Rather it is a compression phenomenon. Air molecules are pushed forward and compressed together (higher air pressure) in the same direction as the wave is moving. This compression then creates areas where there are fewer air particles than normal (lower air pressure). And because a sound wave is a disturbance that is transported through a medium due to the individual elements of the medium interacting, a sound wave is also then a mechanical wave.

Figure 2.2: A Longitudinal Wave

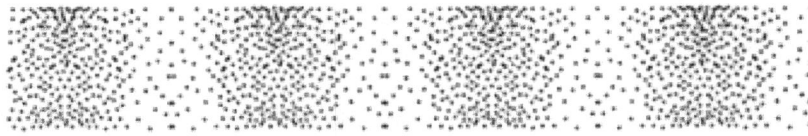

If the pressure waves are caused by something that is repeatedly disturbing the air around it (e.g., a guitar string plucked resulting in a regular vibration pattern) then they are also periodic waves. Air molecules get repeatedly pushed forward and scrunched together (or spread apart) in a regular pattern, resulting in evenly spaced sound waves. If you were to "ride" on a longitudinal wave, your experience would be very different than your experience in a boat. Assume you were moving forward through the air at some normal speed. You might then feel an extra push forward as the wave of more dense air particles hits you, like a push from tailwind. But then you would gradually slow down, until the next wave hit you and pushed you forward again.

The vibrations of a tuning fork can easily create such a mechanical and longitudinal wave. As the tines of the tuning fork vibrate back and forth, they push on and compress neighboring air particles.

Figure 2.3. Vibrating Tuning Fork Creating A Longitudinal Wave

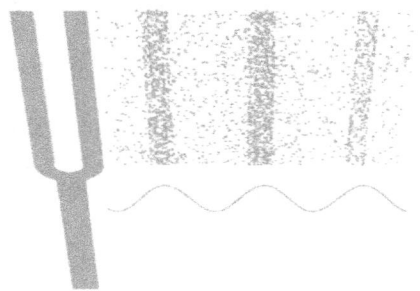

The forward motion of a tine pushes air molecules horizontally to the right and the backward retraction of the tine creates a low-pressure area allowing the air particles to move back to the left. This creates regions in the air where the air particles are scrunched together and other regions where the air particles are spread further apart, known as compressions and rarefactions, respectively. More specifically, the compressions are areas of higher air pressure, while the rarefactions are areas of lower air pressure.

Of course, there is also necessarily a subjective component to sound. Have you ever been asked the question "If a tree falls in the forest and there is no one there to hear it, does it make a sound?" No, it doesn't. The reality is that the air particles originally impacted by the falling of the tree never traveled very far at all—but they did impact the particles next to them, and then those particles impacted the ones next to them, and so on, until the effect "rippled" across the forest to your eardrums. The variations in the air pressure against your eardrums from nearby particles is what you "heard". More specifically, the pressure wave caused the thin membrane of the eardrum to vibrate, starting a process in which the vibrations were eventually converted into electric impulses that your brain interpreted as a specific sound coming from a specific direction.

The tiny variations in air pressure were only the end result of the falling tree. Thus, the subsequent physical (by your ears) and neurological processing and interpretation (by your brain) of those air pressure variations were also essential elements for the "sound" of the falling tree to occur.

One other thing that you should know is that although sound waves are longitudinal waves, it is difficult to represent them in a diagram on paper. Consequently, in discussions of the physics of sound and how it relates to music, sound waves are often represented as "transverse" waves (sine waves) with a wavy line moving across the diagram with clear "peaks" and ""valleys", as might be seen on the screen of an oscilloscope. But it is important to keep in mind that sound waves do not actually work that way.

Figure 2.4: Transverse and Longitudinal Waves

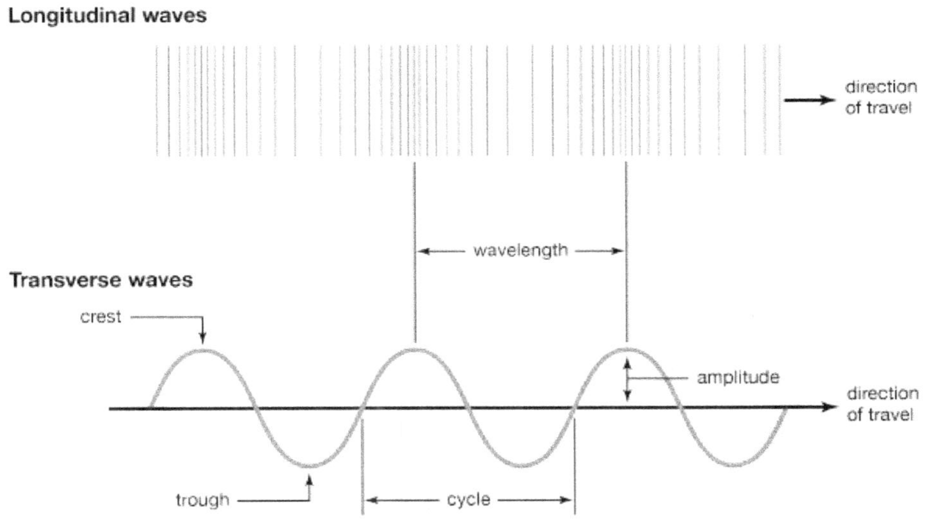

Sound waves also have several special properties, such as: frequency, wavelength, amplitude, and timbre, etc. These are critical to understanding the nature of music.

Frequency

Sound frequency is simply the number of pressure waves (compressions and rarefactions) moving past a set point over some period of time: the greater the number of waves, the higher the frequency. The standard unit of measurement for sound frequency is the Hertz (Hz), where one Hertz is a pressure wave moving past a set point once per second. Humans are able to detect and hear sound frequencies ranging from 20 Hz (twenty waves per second) to 20000 Hz (or 20 kiloHertz) (twenty thousand waves per second).

Wavelength

The distance between the high point in one wave and the high point in the next wave is called the wavelength. In the case of longitudinal waves, the high points are the points at which the air pressure is the highest (compressions). Wavelength is also related to frequency indirectly because if the length of the wave is shorter, the closer the wave peaks are to each other, and so more of them move past a set point over a specific period of time. Consequently, frequency is always higher for shorter wave lengths.

Pitch

Pitch, which is a concept more directly related to music, is simply the "experienced" frequency of a particular set of periodic sound waves (e.g., the sound waves caused by depressing a particular key on a piano keyboard).

Like frequency, pitch can also then be talked about in relative terms. In other words, one pitch can be described as higher or lower relative to a different pitch. The difference in pitches is called an interval, and the most basic interval is the unison, which is simply two identical notes of the same pitch. By comparison, the octave interval is between two pitches where the higher one is exactly twice the frequency of the lower one.

Moreover, frequency and pitch are directly correlated: the greater the frequency of the waves, the higher the pitch.

As we will discuss in the next chapter, notation systems provide a way for musicians and music theorists to communicate with each other more effectively.
For example, different frequencies/pitches can be distinguished by assigning them single alphabetical letters (e.g., A, C, F, or B).

In particular, the frequency of 261.626 Hz is always given the letter designation C. In fact, musicians and others often refer to it as "Middle C". The pitch A, right above middle C, corresponds to exactly 440Hz. What then would be the frequency of the pitch one octave lower than A? The answer is: 220 Hz, and A one octave higher would be 880 Hz. That is because, as mentioned earlier, the upper pitch in an octave is always double the frequency of the lower pitch in the octave. Furthermore, this standardized tuning for the pitch of A above middle C is called the A4 standard or concert pitch (aka, A440), and serves as a reference point, with all other pitches, higher or lower, being set relative to it. In fact, most musical instruments are tuned using this standard frequency for A above middle C as the starting point.

One other important thing keep in mind here is that higher pitched notes have larger frequency differences (in Hertz) between them, but the differences are nevertheless still perceived by humans as an equal change in pitch (one semitone).

Figure 2.5: Chart of Pitches and Corresponding Frequencies in Hertz

NOTE	HZ	NOTE	HZ	NOTE	HZ
A0	27.5000	D3	146.832	G5	783.991
A#0 or Bb0	29.1352	D#3 or Eb3	155.563	G#5 or Ab5	830.609
B0	30.8677	E3	164.814	A5	880.000
C1	32.7032	F3	174.614	A#5 or Bb5	932.328
C#1 or Db1	34.6478	F#3 or Gb3	184.997	B5	987.767
D1	36.7081	G3	195.998	C6	1046.50
D#1 or Eb1	38.8909	G#3 or Ab3	207.652	C#6 or Db6	1108.73
E1	41.2034	A3	220.000	D6	1174.66
F1	43.6535	A#3 or Bb3	233.082	D#6 or Eb6	1244.51
F#1 or Gb1	46.2493	B3	246.942	E6	1318.51
G1	48.9994	C4	261.626	F6	1396.91
G#1 or Ab1	51.9131	C#4 or Db4	277.183	F#6 or Gb6	1479.98
A1	55.0000	D4	293.665	G6	1567.98
A#1 or Bb1	58.2705	D#4 or Eb4	311.127	G#6 or Ab6	1661.22
B1	61.7354	E4	329.628	A6	1760.00
C2	65.4064	F4	349.228	A#6 or Bb6	1864.66
C#2 or Db2	69.2957	F#4 or Gb4	369.994	B6	1975.53
D2	73.4162	G4	391.995	C7	2093.00
D#2 or Eb2	77.7817	G#4 or Ab4	415.305	C#7 or Db7	2217.46
E2	82.4069	A4	440.000	D7	2349.32
F2	87.3071	A#4 or Bb4	466.164	D#7 or Eb7	2489.02
F#2 or Gb2	92.4986	B4	493.883	E7	2637.02
G2	97.9989	C5	523.251	F7	2793.83
G#2 or Ab2	103.826	C#5 or Db5	554.365	F#7 or Gb7	2959.96
A2	110.000	D5	587.330	G7	3135.96
A#2 or Bb2	116.541	D#5 or Eb5	622.254	G#7 or Ab7	3322.44
B2	123.471	E5	659.255	A7	3520.00
C3	130.813	F5	698.456	A#7 or Bb7	3729.31
C#3 or Db3	138.591	F#5 or Gb5	739.989	B7	3951.07
				C8	4186.01

Finally, it should also be pointed out that the assignment of pitches to frequencies can also be somewhat arbitrary. In 1859 France, for example, the same A was tuned to 435

Hz. In the Middle Ages, because people lived far away from each other in isolated communities, tuning could vary widely from place to place. In 1862 the tunings of church bells in various cities throughout Europe were compared, and the result was frequencies for A above middle C ranging from 370 Hz to 567.3 Hz. This was due in part to different materials from which the bells were made, deterioration of the bells over time, as well as the lack of a tuning standard being communicated between the churches. Also, some orchestras tune the A note on their instruments a little sharp, e.g., to 442 Hz or 444 Hz, in order to produce a slightly crisper sound. And as long as all of musicians playing together agree on the special tuning, the music should still sound great. Nevertheless, such differences can still have a noticeable effect on the way music sounds to listeners. In any event, when musicians are talking with each other, it is a lot more effective to communicate that the desired sound is the pitch A4, as opposed to 440Hz.

Amplitude

The high point or "amplitude" of a transverse wave, like a wave on water, is the height of the bounce you get as the wave passes you in your boat: the higher the bounce, the higher the amplitude. As noted earlier, for a longitudinal wave, the highest amplitude (wave peak) is when the air molecules are scrunched together the most, and the lowest amplitude is when there is no scrunching at all, or when rarefaction occurs. This variation in amplitude corresponds to the relative power or energy of the sound waves. We experience these variations as differences in the intensity and volume of the sound. The standard unit of measurement of sound pressure (and intensity) or volume is the decibel (dB), named after Alexander Graham Bell, the inventor of the telephone.

While many typical measuring devices, such as a tape measure, use a linear scale, the measuring scale for decibels is logarithmic, which better represents how changes in sound volume (intensity) effect our ears. To help you better understand this difference, imagine a rope that 80 feet long. If we use linear measurement to compare it to a rope that is 90 feet long, the second rope would be 12.5% longer than the first rope. While comparing the two ropes visually, we could probably see the difference, but it might not seem like much of a difference, especially if we were viewing it from a long distance. However, using logarithmic measurement, a sound that is 90 decibels is only 10 decibels more than a sound that is 80 decibels, but our ears would experience that sound as ten times more intense and powerful than the 80 decibels sound, and nearly twice as loud. When visually comparing an eighty foot rope to a rope that is ten times as long, the longer rope will certainly look significantly longer, even at a distance.

Timbre

Two sounds can have the same pitch, but sound very different, especially if the sound comes from two different musical instruments. These differences are often described using words such as bright, dull, shrill, dark, thin, smooth, murky, brassy, mellow, hollow, full, or breathy, etc. When two pitches are the same, but sound different, these sounds are said to have different timbres. Timbre is also sometimes called "tone," "color," or "tonal color."

For example, a C pitch played on a cello is the same as a C pitch played on an electric guitar, but we perceive the sound very differently because of the different timbres produced by the different instruments. This is because, unlike a tuning fork, the musical sound produced by a musical instrument is way more complex than a single frequency/pitch. Given the way various musical instruments are designed, shaped, constructed, or played, any sound produced with a specific pitch may result in the creation of secondary sounds called "overtones" or harmonics and these additional sounds are added to the original pure pitch sound. It is then that combination of sounds that is actually heard by the listener.

Figure 2.6: The Same Pitch From Different Instruments

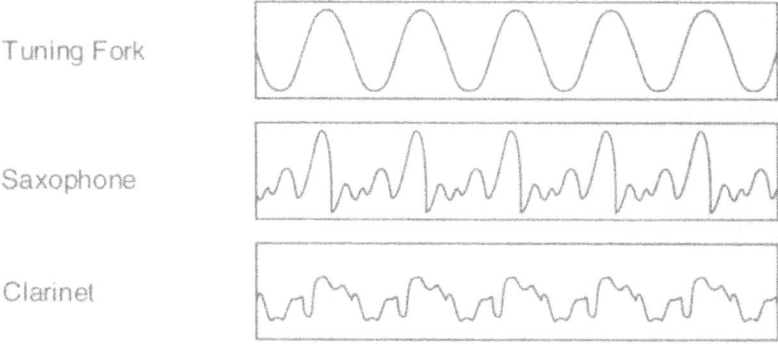

Because of the unique characteristics of a particular type of instrument (e.g., its size, what it is made of, how it is played, or even the acoustic characteristics of the environment in which the sound is produced) what we actually hear may be a whole spectrum of frequencies or pitches so well blended together that they are perceived more or less, as a single frequency.

Timbre may even vary between instruments of the same type due to variations in their construction, and most importantly, the performer's technique. For example, you may have seen trumpet players insert a mute into the bell end of their instrument. Remember how different the trumpet sounds when played this way. The trumpeter has changed the "shape of the sound" or volume of their instrument. Similarly, a vocalist can change the timbre of their voice by the way they shape their mouth or what they do with their tongue while singing.

Harmonics

When a piano string vibrates, the main pitch you hear is the result of the whole string vibrating. If the A key above middle C is played, the string will vibrate back and forth on its full length 440 times a second. That then is the string's fundamental frequency or the first harmonic: 440 times per second. However, when piano strings vibrate, they also vibrate in halves, producing a second harmonic; in thirds, producing a third harmonic; in fourths, producing a fourth harmonic, and so on. These harmonics are produced by vibrations of smaller increments of the string.

And the relationship between the frequencies of a harmonic series is always the same. The second harmonic always has exactly half the wavelength (and twice the frequency) of the fundamental; the third harmonic always has exactly a third of the wavelength (and so three times the frequency) of the fundamental, and so on. A harmonic series can have any note as its first harmonic, so there are many different possible harmonic series.

A column of air vibrating inside a tube, such as a clarinet or a French horn, can also vibrate in halves, thirds, fourths, etc., of the fundamental, so the structure of the harmonic series will be the same. So why then do vibrating strings, clarinets and French horns produce such different timbres?

In any harmonic series, the relative loudness of the different harmonics being produced may vary substantially. For example, when a note is played by a vibrating string, the odd-numbered harmonics may be the strongest; when a clarinet plays the same note, it may be the second, third, and fourth harmonics that are loudest; and when a French horn plays the same note, perhaps the fifth and ninth harmonics are the strongest. When you hear this difference, you are then able to recognize what instrument is playing.

Moreover, the relative loudness of the harmonics also changes from note to note on the same instrument, and this is the difference you hear between the sound of a guitar playing low notes and the same guitar playing high notes.

As I will discuss in a later chapter, natural acoustic harmonics are the basis for another very important musical concept, and one which you likely have heard of before: harmony.

Assume that a singer sings a single note like middle C. Then another singer simultaneously sings a note up one full octave, i.e., twice the frequency of middle C. Given that the second note is a natural harmonic of the first note, the sound waves of the two notes reinforce each other and sound good together. If the second person instead sings a note that is just a bit less than twice the frequency of the first note, the harmonic series of the two notes would not fit together, and the two notes would not sound as good together. In fact, we might even say of the second singer that they were just a bit "off key".

Many combinations of notes share harmonics and so sound good together. When they do, they are considered consonant. For example, two notes with a frequency ratio of 5:4 are said to be separated by an interval of a third and so also sound good when played simultaneously. Other combinations of notes share few harmonics and so are considered dissonant or, when they share no harmonics and really clash, simply "out of tune" with each other.

Chapter 3: Basic Music Notation

> "Music expresses that which cannot be put into words and that which cannot remain silent."
> — *Victor Hugo*

Music, like language, existed for thousands of years before anyone thought to invent a way to write it down so that it could be more easily replicated and passed on to others. Even in modern times, some professional musicians prefer learning and playing music by ear or as improvisation (making it up as they go along), without ever learning to read music or put it in writing. Even some popular and very successful modern singers were not or are not able to read or write music (e.g., Elvis Presley, Michael Jackson, and Taylor Swift). Those who find fault with modern music notation systems rightly point out that, after centuries of extension, elaboration, transformation, and tweaking, the current notation system is neither efficient nor intuitive. In fact, it can be downright confusing.

Nevertheless, without written music, we would not be able to experience the sheer complexity of the music of Mozart, be awed by the New York Philharmonic playing the William Tell Overture, or learn the tune to the Star Spangled Banner. It is a lot easier to study, share, replicate, perform, and discuss music when it has been written down. As this book delves deeper into music theory, it will often be necessary, for the sake of clarity, to represent musical concepts and procedures as they might be communicated to a musician via sheet music. Consequently, having a basic understanding of musical notation should help you get the most out of this book.

Common Notation

The generally accepted method of music notation, called common notation, begins with the staff, which is five horizontal lines that are evenly spaced vertically.

Figure 3.1: The Musical Staff

Vertical lines called "bar line" are also added to divide up the staff into short sections called "measures" (or bars). A double-bar vertical line, sometimes with both a heavy bar and a light bar, marks out larger sections of a musical work, with a heavy double-bar vertical line always used to indicate the very end of a piece of music.

Figure 3.2: The Musical Staff with Bar Lines

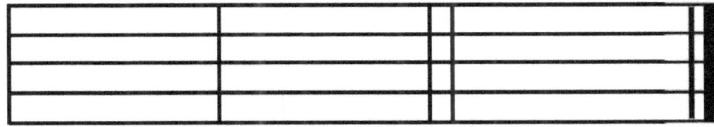

Each of the five lines and four spaces on the staff can also be assigned a specific letter. For example, under certain circumstances, starting with the bottom line, the letters assigned could be E, G, B, D, and F. Similarly, starting with the bottom space, the spaces could be designated as F, A, C, and E. Notice also that as you move from the bottom of the staff to the top, the letters assigned to the lines and spaces would be in alphabetical order, E, F, G, and then A, B, C, D, E, and F.

Figure 3.3: Letters For Lines and Spaces on Staff

On the staff as a whole, on the lines, in the spaces between the lines, or in the space above or below the staff, many different kinds of symbols can be written to tell the musician various things about how to play the music. These include the basic components of the music itself: note symbols (sounds) and rest symbols (silences). Other symbols on the staff include clef symbols, the key signature, the time signature, tempo markings, dynamic markings, repeats, and accent symbols. Three of the most important symbols on the staff, the clef symbol, the key signature, and the time signature, will always appear at the beginning of the staff.

Figure 3.4: A Musical Staff with Symbols

Musical Notes

One of the most important symbols placed on a staff are, of course, the musical "notes," and they can have up to three parts: the head, which is the round part of the note; a stem, which is a semi-vertical line extending up (or down) from the head; and sometimes a flag, which is a short wavy line extending out from the stem, like a flag on a flagpole.

Furthermore, sometimes the head is solidly filled in, and in some cases, it has an open space in the middle.

More importantly, the notes tell a musician to make a particular sound at a specific pitch and for a particular duration. Usually, the pitch to be played by the musician is indicated by which line or in what space the note is written. For example, a note symbol written on the bottom line would indicate that the musician should play a sound with the pitch E, while a note symbol written in the third space from the bottom of the staff would instruct the musician to play a sound with the pitch of C. The length of time for which the sound is to be played is indicated by the type of note symbol used, e.g., whole notes, half notes, quarter notes, etc.

Figure 3.5: Notes on the Musical Staff

Without getting into the actual temporal length of a whole note, what is most important to know at this point is that as the name implies, a half note is played for half the time that a whole note is played, and a quarter note is played for one quarter the length of time of a whole note, and so on. Quarter notes, eighth notes, and sixteenth notes are the only notes with solid heads, and eighth and sixteenth notes are the only notes that have flags—one flag for an eighth note (quaver) and two flags for a sixteenth note (semi-quaver). Both whole notes and half notes have heads with an empty space in them, but of these two, only half notes have a stem.

Figure 3.6: Symbols for Musical Notes

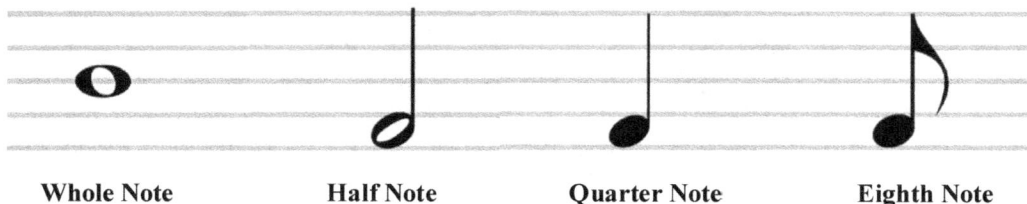

     Whole Note   **Half Note**   **Quarter Note**   **Eighth Note**

Notes with stems can also have their stems extend upward above the head or extend downward below the head. This variation has no implications for the music being played and is only done when the note is so close to the top of the staff that its stem would extend up beyond the top of the staff. Purely for clarity and stylistic purposes, the stem is pointed downward so that it remains entirely on the staff.

Notes that have flags on their stems (whether the stems are pointed up or down) can also be connected to each other using "beams" or "ligatures." This is often done when two such notes that are the same duration occur one after the other. The flags on the two notes are removed and replaced with a beam that connects the tops of the stems of the two notes.

Figure 3.7: Notes with Beams Instead of Flags

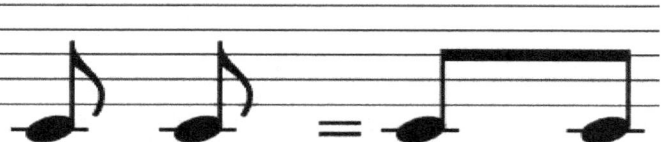

If there are four of the same duration of notes in a sequence, they can also be separated into two groups, with each group of two connected by a double beam. Even a group of four such notes can be connected by a double beam. However, one important thing to keep in mind here is that the notes being connected in this way do not need to be the same pitch, only the same duration. In other words, an eighth note for a C and an eighth note for E that follows it, can still be connected using a beam. Using beams instead of flags also really has no implication for the music being played. It is also done simply to make the musical notation look less messy.

For any piece of music, multiple note symbols will be placed on the staff, and since music notation is always read from left to right, the order in which the notes appear on the the staff tells the musician the order in which they are to be played.

The notes that are identified by their positioning on the lines or spaces of the staff are called "natural notes".

Sharps and Flats

When you compare the interval between two adjacent natural notes, you will see that the distance is not always the same. In fact, some pairs of notes are twice as far away from each other when compared to other pairs of notes. The interval in frequency/pitch between those notes that are furthest apart is called a whole step or whole tone. In contrast, the interval between those notes that are closest together is called a half step or semitone. In Western music, additional notes are added between the natural notes that are a full step apart. These are called sharp notes and flat notes. In fact, on a piano keyboard, black keys were added between some of the white keys to make playing these notes possible on the piano. This has the effect then making all musical notes exactly one-half step apart.

It is also important to remember that calling the notes sharps and flats does not necessarily imply the corresponding pitches somehow have a "sharper" or "flatter" sounding timbre. Over centuries of music study, these names have just become the conventional way of referring to these notes.

Figure 3.8: Flat and Sharp Notes

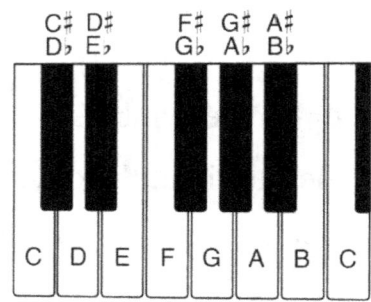

A sharp note is one half step higher than the natural note next to it. On the staff, it can be designated by the symbol "superscript #" placed next to the letter for that note, e.g. $F^\#$. The new note is called F sharp.

A flat note is one half step lower than the natural note next to it and it is designated by the symbol "superscript italic b" placed next to the letter for that note, e.g., B^b. The new note is called B flat.

On a piano keyboard, the white keys play the natural notes, e.g., A, G, B, etc. The black keys play the sharp and flat notes, e.g., F sharp or B Flat. So, the distance between any key on a piano and a key next to it, whether white or black, is a half step or semitone.

In any octave, there are five sharp and flat notes: $A^\#/B^b$, $C^\#/D^b$, $D^\#/E^b$, $F^\#/G^b$, and $G^\#/A^b$. Notice also that there are no sharps or flats between B and C or between E and F. That is because those notes were already one-half step apart and so there was no need to add additional notes between them.

You may have also noticed that adjacent sharps and flats are exactly the same note, just with different names, e.g., G sharp and A flat. These are called enharmonic notes. And if you were to play these notes on a piano keyboard, you would use exactly the same black key to play both of them. So why give them different names? Whether you call the note a G sharp or an A flat isn't just arbitrary. It can communicate important information about how the note functions as the music progresses. Remember, music progresses linearly over time, so a G sharp or A flat may sound completely different in the context of what notes are played before it, with it (as part of a chord), or after it.

For example, if your music includes a sequence of notes increasing in pitch (moving higher), and the sequence is to include a C sharp/D flat, it would make more sense to label the note as C sharp instead of D flat, so as to more accurately indicate that the notes are to continue ascending. Similarly, when the sequence of notes is descending in pitch, it would make more sense to label the note as D flat since that is more consistent with a continuation of the descent.

Octaves

Given that there are seven notes with letter names (A, B, C, D, E, F, and G), adding five sharp/flat combinations ($A^{\#}/B^{b}$, $C^{\#}/D^{b}$, $D^{\#}/E^{b}$, $F^{\#}/G^{b}$, $G^{\#}/A^{b}$), results in twelve distinctive notes. These twelve notes collectively are called an octave or register, and the notes are the same for every octave, just at higher or lower pitches. And, as noted earlier, when two notes are exactly one octave apart, the frequency of the higher one is always that of the lower one.

Also, pitches of the twelve notes in an octave are always exactly one semitone (half step) apart. In fact, if we take the frequency any note in an octave and multiply it by exactly 1.0595, the result will be the frequency of the next higher note in the octave. This number is called the "twelve root of 2" because if you multiply it by itself twelve times, the result is exactly two (and so the frequency/pitch highest note in an octave is exactly twice that of the lowest note).
This method of dividing the octave into twelve equal intervals is known as equal temperament tuning, and this will be discussed in more detail later later.

Around fifty years ago, the Acoustical Society of America introduced a register designation system based upon the layout of the standard piano keyboard. Specifically, the designation system begins with the first C note (and the octave based on it) leftmost on the piano keyboard, and extends up to (and including) the last B note seven octaves above it on the far right of the keyboard. Each octave in between is designated by a letter of the note that begins that octave, e.g. C, followed by a subscript number denoting the number of the octave within which that pitch resides, from lowest to highest (left to right on the keyboard). For example, the first C octave on the left would be C_1, the second C_2, and so on.

However, there are actually three keys on a standard piano keyboard to the left of the first C octave (C_1). These notes are labeled in two ways: A_0, B^b_0, B_0, or simply A, B^b, B. And C_8 contains only one note, a very high C, and so it does not actually represent a full octave. The entire piano keyboard then spans the range from A_0 to C_8.

Of course, musical instruments can play, and human ears can hear, musical notes from more than one octave. Pianos, for example, with eighty-eight keys on a full-size keyboard, can play as many as seven octaves, as indicated above.

However, human ears, human voices, and musical instruments also have limits, and so there is a limited number of octaves available for music. Humans can hear a range of around ten octaves. However, seven of those octaves cover the bottom eighth of the range, from 20 Hz up to 2500 Hz, which corresponds roughly to the pitch range from E^b_0 to E^b_7, which is slightly lower than the lowest pitch on a piano. Only the piano, harp and piccolo can go higher than E^b_7, and not by very much. The bottom note on a double bass or bass guitar, E_1, has a frequency of just over 40 Hz. Only the harp, piano, double bassoon, and organ can go below this. Even the best professional singers can usually perform only over a range of one and a half to just over two octaves.

The Chromatic Scale

The group of all possible musical notes is called the Chromatic Scale. Chromatic comes from the Greek word *chrôma*, meaning color. The chromatic scale is then the group of "'notes with all possible colors".

Every octave will always contain the same group of twelve possible notes (just at different pitches or in a different order). It doesn't matter which octave is being discussed or on what note the octave begins. In this sense, then, all octaves are identical. Since the octave and a Chromatic scale both contain the group of possible notes, they are in effect then the same thing, and there is only one Chromatic scale. Nevertheless, understanding the concept of the Chromatic Scale will become important for topics I will discuss later in this book.

The Clef

At the leftmost end of every staff is a clef symbol. There are basically two different types of clef symbols in common music notation, the "treble clef" (sometimes also called a G clef) and the "bass clef" (sometimes called the F clef). Each serves as a kind of decoding key to tell you how to interpret what follows on the rest of the staff. More specifically, the clef tells you how to interpret the note symbols on the lines and in the spaces of the staff.

For example, a treble clef symbol tells you that the second line from the bottom (the line that the symbol curls around) is "G". Since the note letters follow alphabetically as you move up the staff, that means that, as we mentioned before, the notes on the lines of the staff for a treble clef are E, G, B, D, and F, while the spaces are F, A, C, and E.

Figure 3.9: The Treble Clef

A bass clef symbol tells you that the second line from the top (the one bracketed by the symbol's dots) is an F note. The notes are still arranged in ascending alphabetical order, but they are all in different places than they were on the treble clef. So the lowermost line is a G note, followed by a B, D, F, and then an A, as you move up the staff, and the spaces are then A, C, E, and G.

Figure 3.10: The Bass Clef

The notes that appear on the Treble clef staff are those usually played by the right hand of a pianist, while those on the Bass clef are typically played by the left hand of the pianist. Similarly, notes on the bass clef are those usually played by deeper sounding musical instruments such as bassoons, tubas, cellos, bass guitars, and bass and baritone voices. In contrast, notes on a Treble clef staff are played by instruments such as flutes, piccolos, violins, soprano saxophones, and soprano voices.

The positioning of the notes on the two different staffs for treble and base clefs, which never changes, is such a fundamental concept in writing and reading music, that students are often taught mnemonics (memory aides) to help them learn and remember those relative positions. For example, as a way of remembering the notes on the lines of a treble clef staff, you can learn and remember the phrase "Every Good Boy Deserves Fudge". The first letters of each of these words E, G, B, D and F are then the letters corresponding to the lines on the staff. Similarly, if you just learn and remember the word FACE, that should help you remember the notes in the spaces of the treble clef staff, because the letters for the notes spell out that word as you move up the staff.

For the bass clef staff, a helpful mnemonic for remembering the notes on the lines might be "Good Boys Do Fine Always", and for the notes in the spaces it could be "All Cows Eat Grass".

Music may also be written on multiple staves (plural of staff), especially when the different staves are to be played by the same musician simultaneously (left and right hand for a pianist) or by different musicians (members of a band or orchestra). More specifically, there will be a Treble clef staff at the top, and a Bass clef staff beneath it, joined together along the left side by a long vertical bar.

This is called a grand staff. And if we were to create a short additional line between the two staves (a ledger line), thus creating a single staff with 11 lines, the musical note commonly referred to as "Middle-C" is one line below the E on the bottom line of the Treble clef staff. Similarly, the A on the top line of the Bass clef staff is the A note one line below middle-C. And the spaces just below and above middle-C would be B and D notes, respectively.

Figure 3.11: The Grand Staff

Together, the Treble and Bass clefs cover most of the notes that are in the range of musical instruments and human voices.

Chapter 4: Intervals

"I would say that music is the easiest means in which to express, but since words are my talent, I must try to express clumsily in words what the pure music would have done better."
— *William Faulkner*

As previously mentioned, an interval is the distance between any two pitches or notes, e.g., how much lower or higher one note is when compared to the other note. So if you pick any note and then play any other note above or below it, either simultaneously or in succession, the difference between the two notes in pitch is an interval.

The concept of an interval is so important for music and music theory that it would be difficult, if not impossible, to discuss other important music concepts such as scales, chords, harmonic progression, cadence, and consonance and dissonance, without first explaining intervals. In fact, intervals are used by musicians to build scales, chords (or harmonies), and melodies. It might be argued that beyond notes themselves, intervals are the single most important building block of music.

Moreover, while it is certainly important to understand intervals on a conceptual level—what they are, how they differ, how they work, etc.— for musicians and others it will also be important to understand them in practice. Each interval has a unique sound, especially when the two notes are played simultaneously, and it can be a very valuable skill as a musician to be able to identify musical intervals by ear. Therefore, as I discuss intervals conceptually, I encourage you to locate them on a piano keyboard and play them out loud, so you can hear how they sound, get to know them, learn how they differ, learn which ones sound good and which ones do not, understand how they relate to each other, and learn how to use them creatively.

We already know that an octave is an interval. However, there are also 12 distinct notes within an octave, and so any pair of notes in that octave are also separated by an interval. Furthermore, any interval that is twelve or fewer semitones is called a simple interval. So there are many possible simple intervals in just one octave, In fact, in any given octave, there are technically 144 possible pairs of notes, e.g., C and C, C and D, C and E, C and F, etc., and so at least 144 possible intervals.

However, only certain pairs of these notes sound well together, either simultaneously or in succession, and so these are the intervals that are most important for musicians. In this chapter, I will introduce you to the most important and most commonly used intervals. I will not be discussing all of the possible intervals in an octave.

Interval Characteristics

Melodic or Harmonic. One important characteristic of an interval is whether it is harmonic or melodic. An interval is vertical, or harmonic, if the two notes are heard simultaneously, such as in a chord. In contrast, an interval is horizontal, or melodic if the notes are heard successively.

Ascending or Descending. Melodic intervals can also be either ascending or descending. An ascending interval is when a note lower in pitch is followed by higher note, for example C to D#. In contrast, an interval is descending when a higher note is followed by a lower note, e.g. F to C. Obviously, when intervals are harmonic, direction doesn't matter.

Any given octave, then, also contains 144 possible descending interval pairs in addition to the 144 possible ascending interval pairs.

Also, when an interval is ascending, and when necessary, sharp (#) symbols will be used. However, when the interval is descending, you will use flat (b) symbols where appropriate.

Width or Height. The width or height of an interval can be described in terms of relative pitch, e.g., A or B, or the number of semitones (half steps) or full tones (full steps) between the two notes. However, for music theorists, there are two other common ways of describing the width or height of the interval.

One approach is to use the small-integer ratio of the frequencies between the two notes, such as 2:1 for an octave. When intervals can be described in this way, they are called pure intervals.

However, this can be a bit misleading. Even though the human ear perceives a 2:1 ratio in pitch as a linear increase (difference), it really is not. In fact, successive increments of increase in pitch by the same interval, (e.g. steps or semitones) actually results in an exponential increase of frequency. Consequently, intervals are also often measured in cents, a unit derived from the logarithm of the frequency ratio.

When frequency is expressed in a logarithmic scale, the distance between a given frequency and its double (an octave) is divided into 1200 equal parts. Each of these parts is one cent. In the current tuning system used for most musical instruments, called twelve-tone equal temperament (12-TET), all semitones have exactly the same size. Since there are twelve semitones in an octave, each one is thus 100 cents in size. In other words, one cent can be also defined as one one-hundredth of a semitone.

Using the logarithmic measurement unit cents is not just an arbitrary approach to measuring intervals. Because 12-TET is the commonly used basis for tuning musical instruments, the size of most equal-tempered intervals cannot be expressed by small-integer ratios, although it is very close to the size of the corresponding intervals. For instance, an equal-tempered interval of five semitones has a frequency ratio of $2^{7/12}:1$, approximately equal to 1.498:1, or 2.997:2, very close to 3:2, but not exactly 3:2.

Diatonic or Chromatic. Another important way of distinguishing between intervals is whether they are chromatic (Greek: χρωματική) or diatonic (Greek: διατονική). As I will discuss in more detail in the next chapter, the chromatic scale is a group containing all possible notes in any octave (naturals, as well as sharps and flats). A chromatic interval, then, is an interval formed between two notes of a chromatic scale.

In contrast, diatonic intervals are a subset of the chromatic intervals. Specifically, they are the intervals between pairs of the seven natural notes from the chromatic scale (the white keys on a piano keyboard). In other words, all diatonic intervals are also chromatic intervals, but not all chromatic intervals are diatonic intervals. Since there are 49 possible pairs of seven notes, there are 49 ascending diatonic intervals as well as 49 descending diatonic intervals.

Most importantly, as will be also discussed in more detail in the next chapter, diatonic intervals are also a special group of intervals which make up the Major scale.

Named Intervals

Because many intervals have shared characteristics, another common way of describing them is to assign them to groups based on their similarities and then give the groups names. This provides an easier way for musicians and others to understand them, distinguish them, and discuss them.

The most common naming scheme for intervals is based on two properties of the interval: the number (unison, second, third, etc.) and the quality (perfect, major, minor, augmented, diminished).

More specifically, the number (also called the diatonic number) refers to the number of natural notes between and including the upper and lower notes in the interval, regardless of whether the interval is ascending or descending. On the other hand, quality is based in part on how many actual semitones or half-steps make up the interval and how it is constructed.

Number. The number of an interval is the number of diatonic note names or positions (lines and spaces) on the musical staff it encompasses, including the positions of both notes forming the interval.

For example, if you count the staff lines for B and D and the space between them, the result is two lines and one space. The total is then three. So the interval would be called "a third." Similarly, the interval between A and F is a "sixth," because there are two lines and four spaces (total of six) separating them. The interval C–G is a "fifth" because the notes from C to the G above it encompass five letter names (C, D, E, F, G) and occupy five consecutive staff positions, including the positions of C and G. That is how the "number" part of an interval name is operationalized. But what about the "quality" part of the name?

Quality. Intervals can be either: perfect (P), major (M), minor (m), augmented (A), or diminished (d). Double augmented and double diminished intervals are rare but also possible. It should also be noted that when discussing intervals, the terms: "Major" and "Perfect" are usually capitalized, while "minor" is not. Major and minor intervals are used frequently in Western music, while Perfect intervals are more common in ethnic music from other cultures.

Perfect Intervals

What makes these particular intervals perfect? Perfect intervals are always natural to natural, sharp to sharp, and flat to flat. In other words, no matter what the distance is between the bottom and top notes of an interval, they will always begin and end on the same type of note.

Another thing that makes them perfect intervals is that the notes are very closely related to each other, and so are highly consonant (sound particularly good together). In fact, for listeners, that consonance is easily perceived and remembered.

As will be discussed later, such notes can also described as sensory consonant. In contrast, Major, minor, augmented or diminished intervals are typically considered less consonant or more dissonant.

Unison. When two identical notes are played by the same type of instrument or different instruments simultaneously, or in succession, that is an interval called perfect unison. The interval can be called a Perfect 1st (P1). If played by the same instruments, and those instruments are both properly tuned, the sounds produced by the two instruments should be indistinguishable.

Octaves. All octave intervals are also perfect and thus can be identified as a Perfect 8th (P8) interval. First, they also always begin and end not only on the same type of note, but in fact end on the same note, just at a higher pitch. Also, the two notes that begin and end an octave, will always sound especially good together, whether played simultaneously or successively.

Fourths. Most fourths are perfect intervals (P4), spanning five semitones (500 cents), with two exceptions. The two exceptions will be discussed later. Until the late 19th century, the perfect fourth was also often called by its Greek name: diatessaron.

For example, the interval of middle C up to F is a perfect fourth. We know it is a fourth because C and F are separated from each other on the musical staff by exactly four lines and spaces. More importantly, C and F are five semitones apart, corresponding to C-$C^{\#}/D_b$, $C^{\#}/D_b$-D, D-$D^{\#}/E_b$, $D^{\#}/E_b$-E, and E-F. A perfect fourth always corresponds to a small number pitch ratio of 4:3, or about 498 cents, while in equal temperament, a perfect fourth is equal to five semitones, or 500 cents. Please remember that when counting the quantity of steps or half steps/semitones separating two notes in an interval, always count the spaces between the notes and not the notes themselves.

Similarly, the interval from D to G is a perfect fourth. We know it is a fourth because D and G are separated from each other on the musical staff by exactly four lines and spaces. But is a perfect fourth? The notes actually contained in the interval are D, $D^{\#}/E_b$, E, F, $F^{\#}/G_b$, and G. That is five semitones separating the notes in the interval. So yes, D to G is also a perfect fourth.

One example of a perfect fourth is the beginning of the "Bridal Chorus" from Wagner's Lohengrin ("Treulich geführt"). You know this song as "Here Comes the Bride"). Other examples are the first two notes of the Christmas carol "Hark! The Herald Angels Sing" and, for a descending perfect fourth, the second and third notes of "O Come All Ye Faithful".

Fifths. Most fifths are also perfect intervals spanning seven semitones (700 cents). Until the late 19th century, they were often also referred to by a Greek name: diapente.

For example, the interval of middle C to G is a perfect fifth. We know it is a fifth because C and G are separated from each other on the musical staff by exactly three lines and two spaces. More importantly, C and G are seven semitones apart, corresponding to C-C#/Db, C#/Db-D, D-D#/Eb, D#/Eb-E, E-F, F-F#/Gb, and F#/Gb-G. A perfect fifth always corresponds to a small number pitch ratio of 3:2, or about 701.955 cents, while in equal temperament a perfect fifth is equal to seven semitones, or 700 cents.

Similarly, the interval E to B is also a perfect fifth. We know it is a fifth because E and B are separated from each other on the musical staff by exactly three lines and two spaces. But is it a perfect fifth? In fact, E and B are seven semitones apart, corresponding to E-F, F-F#/Gb, F#/Gb-G, G-G#/Ab, G#/Ab-A, A-A#/Bb, and A#/Bb-B. So yes, E to B is also a perfect fifth.

The perfect fifth is typically considered more consonant than any other interval except the unison and the octave. In other words, the notes of a perfect fifth sound really good together whether played simultaneously or in succession.

One example of a perfect fifth is at the start of "Twinkle, Twinkle, Little Star". The pitch of the second "twinkle" is a perfect fifth above the pitch of the first "twinkle".

Major and minor Intervals

Major. Major (diatonic) intervals are those which are part of the major scale. A Major scale interval can only be a second, third, sixth, or seventh, and Major intervals are labeled with a large "M."

Some examples of major intervals include: Major 2nd (C to D), Major 3rd (C to E), Major 6th (C to A), Major 7th (C to B).

Minor. The notes in minor scales are the same as in the major scales, as well as most other diatonic scales. However, a minor interval is always one half step smaller than the corresponding Major interval. For example, the minor 3rd is one semitone below the Major 3rd (C to E_b rather than C to E). Also, minor intervals are labeled with a small "m."

Some examples of minor intervals include: minor 2nd (C to C#/Db), minor 3rd (C to D#/Eb), minor 6th (C to G#/Ab), and minor 7th (C to A#/Bb).

Seconds. If an interval involves one natural note (C) and only one semitone of separation. It is a minor 2nd.

In contrast, the interval C to D involves two natural notes, but also two semitones of separation. It is a Major 2nd.

Thirds. If an interval involves two adjacent natural notes, (e.g. C-D) but three semitones of separation, it is a minor 3rd. However, with three natural notes and four semitones, it is a Major 3rd.

Sixths. If the interval involves five natural notes and eight semitones of separation, it is a minor 6th. In contrast, six natural notes and nine semitone separation would be a Major 6th.

Sevenths. Six natural notes and ten semitones of separation would constitute a minor 7th, whereas seven natural notes and 11 semitones of separation would the be a Major 7th.

Augmented or Diminished Intervals

If an interval is artificially made a half-step larger than a perfect or a major interval, it is called an augmented interval. In contrast, an interval that is artificially made a half-step smaller than a perfect or a minor interval is called a diminished interval. This can be done to any type of interval, except a unison obviously cannot be diminished. It is typically done when the result would be a new set of notes that will sound better together. But not all augmented or diminished intervals will sound good.

For augmented intervals, despite being one semitone larger, the interval number does not change. Augmented intervals are identified with an "A", the abbreviation "Aug.", or a "+" preceding the number. If the P5 from C to G were changed to a C to $G^\#$, it would become an augmented 5th, or +5.

For example, there is a 4th between C and $F^\#$ (C-$C^\#$/D_b-D-$D^\#$/E_b-E-F-$F^\#$) that is created artificially by adding an additional semitone ($F^\#$) to the perfect 4th note sequence of five notes/semitones. This is called an augmented fourth interval (A4). The result is that while it still contains the same four natural notes (C-D-E-F) of a perfect fourth, it is not a perfect fourth, because in its augmented form, it actually contains six semitones (600 cents), and not the usual five of a perfect 4th.

Similarly, a Major 3rd such as C-E can be augmented by adding an additional semitone resulting in C–$E^\#$. This would then be an augmented Major 3rd, or A3.

An example of an augmented 5th would be interval produced by adding a single semitone to a perfect 5th. For example, as mentioned earlier, the interval from C to G is a perfect 5th, seven semitones wide. However, C^b to G, and from C to $G\#$ are augmented fifths, each containing eight semitones.

Diminished intervals are created when a perfect or minor interval is made one half step smaller and again the interval number is not changed. Diminished intervals can be labeled with a "d," the abbreviations "dim" or "deg," or a "°". . If the perfect fifth from C to G above were changed to a C to G♭, the interval would become a diminished 5th, or dim 5.

For example, the interval between C and Gb (C-D-E-F-Gb) is artificially created by removing a semitone from a perfect fifth note sequence. This is called a diminished fifth (d5). The result is that while it is still considered a fifth, it is not a perfect fifth, because in its diminished form, it actually contains only six semitones (600 cents), not usual seven of a perfect fifth.

Similarly, a third such as C♯–E♭, which spans two semitones, falls short of a minor 3rd (C–E♭) by one semitone. It is therefore a diminished minor third.

Of course, one can also create a fifth by diminishing a minor sixth, e.g., C to G#/Ab. Diminishing the final note by one half step yields an interval from C to G, which then is the equivalent of a fifth, because it contains the notes C, D, E, F, and G.

It should also be noted that seconds, thirds, sixths, and sevenths can only be diminished if the interval is decreased by two half steps by using a "double flat," which is sometimes needed to write an augmented or diminished interval correctly. However, even under such circumstances, it is still the actual distance in half steps between the notes that determines the type of interval, not whether the notes are written as natural, sharp, or double-sharp. So the interval number still does not change.

Diminished and Augmented intervals are also always enharmonically equivalent to their Major, minor, and Perfect interval counterparts – they are the same distance in terms of natural notes, but just have different names. So an augmented fourth and a diminished fifth are both equivalent to a fourth because they both contain just four natural notes (two lines and two spaces).

Similarly, a diminished 4th and Major 3rd are physically (distance-wise) the same intervals. The name that will be used for intervals often depends on how the interval is being used, e.g., in a scale or chord. More on this later.

Finally, you should have also recognized the augmented fourth between C and F♯ and the diminished fifth between C and G♭ are also enharmonically equivalent intervals. That is because the added notes F# and Gb are just enharmonic spellings of the same note, essentially added to the C-F sequence of notes. In fact, as mentioned above, the diminished fifth and augmented fourth sound exactly the same.

The Tritone Interval

Any interval with a width of six semitones is also often called a Tritone. This is because two semitones equal one tone, so six semitones equal three tones. In Western Music, this unique interval, which cannot be spelled as a major, minor, or perfect interval, is especially tense and dissonant and creates a sound that feels particularly in need of resolution. By this analysis, both the augmented fourth interval and the diminished fifth interval discussed earlier are also Tritone intervals because they both span six semitones.

Figure 4.1 shows the most important intervals, and assumes the root note is middle C. However, it is important to keep in mind that the root note can be any note, but the relative characteristics for the intervals will not change.

Figure 4.1: Common Intervals

Notes	Interval Name	Width in Semitones
C-C	Perfect 1st (Unison)	0
C-C$^\#$/D^b	minor 2nd	1
C-D	Major 2nd	2
C-D$^\#$/E^b	minor 3rd	3
C-E	Major 3rd	4
C-F	Perfect 4th	5
C-F$^\#$/G^b	Tritone	6
C-G	Perfect 5th	7
C-G$^\#$/A^b	minor 6th	8
C-A	Major 6th	9
C-A$^\#$/B^b	minor 7th	10
C-B	Major 7th	11
C-C$_2$	Perfect 8th (octave)	12

Thus, there are 4 basic Major intervals, 4 basic minor intervals, 4 basic Perfect intervals, and the Tritone interval, which corresponds to the Augmented 4th or diminished 5th.

Interval Inversion

Any interval can also be inverted. This basically involves moving the lowest note in an interval to one or more octaves higher (or moving the highest note to one or more octaves lower). Thus, the higher note becomes the lower note and vice versa. The result is a completely different interval. For example, if we invert the interval C-G - a perfect fifth—and move C one octave higher-the result is perfect fourth G-C. Similarly, if we invert C-E a Major third—the result is minor 6th E-C.

There are, however, several points to keep in mind regarding interval inversion.

First, a descending interval is not an inverted interval. These two concepts are often confused.

Second, it is standard practice to name an interval based on the lowest note in the interval. So when the lowest note is changed through inversion, the name of the interval necessarily changes also.

Also, there is no rule as to which note is flipped. For example, for interval C-E, there are clearly two choices: The lower note, e.g., C, is moved to the octave above the E, or the higher note, E, is moved an octave below the C. The choice is often made for purely creative reasons.

It may also be helpful to remember that seconds always invert to sevenths, thirds to sixths, and so forth. And the fact that each of these pairs will always add up to nine. This is known to music theorists as "the rule of nines.". It might even be useful at times, to think of intervals as coming in pairs—one up and one down.

Finally, the inversion of a perfect interval always results in a perfect interval. In contrast, the inversion of a major interval is a minor interval, the inversion if a minor interval is a Major, and the inversion of an augmented interval is a diminished interval.

These ideas, when taken together, can become very important when you are trying to identify an interval, especially a descending one, or one that has been inverted. To identify the new interval, just subtract the number of the old interval from 9. For example, if the original interval was a Major third, the inversion will be a minor 6th. This is because 9-3 = 6, and a Major always inverts to a minor.

But why is inverting intervals important? Occasionally, musicians want to use a musical technique called counterpoint in their compositions. Using an inverted interval is one way in which this can be done. But musicians also want to achieve consonance as much as possible. In other words, they want the counterpoint to fit well and sound good in relation to the rest of the music. Having an awareness of how intervals invert will help in creating a counterpoint that will also follow all rules of consonance and dissonance. For example, a perfect fifth is consonant, but its inversion, a perfect fourth is not.

Simple and Compound Intervals

A simple interval is an interval spanning at most one octave. However, a compound interval includes two or more intervals that span more than one octave. For example, if you start with a Major 3rd, and add a Major 7th, the result is a Major 10th. Similarly, adding a minor 6th to a minor 7th results in a minor 13th. And you can also reverse the process, and decompose a compound interval into one or more octaves plus a simple interval. A major seventeenth, for example, can be decomposed into two octaves and one major third.

When creating a compound interval, the quality will be the same as the quality of the simple interval on which it is based. For example, any compound interval combining a Major 3rd and one or more Perfect 8ths (octaves) would also be a Major —- e.g., a Major 10th $(1+(8-1)+(3-1) = 10)$, or a Major 17th $(1+(8-1)+(8-1)+(3-1) = 17)$.

Similarly, combining a Perfect 5th with one or more a Perfect 8ths would yield a perfect twelfth $(1+(8-1)+(5-1) = 12)$ or a perfect nineteenth $(1+(8-1)+(8-1)+(5-1) = 19)$.

Notice that two combined octaves result in a fifteenth, not a sixteenth $(1+(8-1)+(8-1) = 15)$. Similarly, three octaves combined are a twenty-second $(1+3\times(8-1) = 22)$, and so on.

Enharmonic Intervals

Enharmonic intervals are intervals that sound the same but are "spelled" differently. They have the alternative names depending upon the enharmonic spelling of the particular notes contained within them.

The most common enharmonic intervals are the diminished fifth and the augmented fourth. However they are not the only intervals that can be "spelled" in more than one way. A major third can also be written as a diminished fourth or a minor second can be written as an augmented unison. Composers usually have good reasons for "spelling" an interval in a particular way, so you should always follow their lead.

Consonance and Dissonance

Traditionally, consonance refers to notes that sound good together and is associated with sweetness and pleasantness. In contrast, dissonance refers to notes that don't sound good together and is associated with harshness and unpleasantness. As was discussed in Chapter 2, overtones or harmonics (partials) generated by various types of musical instruments, can either sound pleasant in relation to their fundamental, or they can sound unpleasant. Specifically, those harmonics that have certain ratios relative to the fundamental will sound good. Those harmonics might then be said to be consonant with their fundamental sound. This means that on some level there is a clear objective quality to the concepts of consonance and dissonance based in the physics of sound.

With regard to intervals, consonance (or concord) is the quality that is perceived as stable and complete in itself. These intervals require no resolution. The consonant intervals are P1, P4, m3, M3, P5, M6, m6, and P8.

All other intervals within the octave are considered dissonant. Dissonant intervals feel incomplete and are perceived as creating tension that requires resolution to more consonant intervals.

However, it is also important to note that consonance and dissonance also clearly involve subjective qualities as well. Consequently, discussions that imply that "consonance" is always "good" and "dissonance always "bad" are misleading.
What one person finds displeasingly dissonant, another may find exciting and interesting. Similarly, variables such as musical genre, timbre and tone, and the context where the music is being performed can all influence the perceived consonance and dissonance of musical pieces.

Because consonance and dissonance are dependent on the perceptions of listeners, they are then subjective qualities of intervals that can vary widely between individual, between different cultures, and at different points in history.

Additionally, both consonance and dissonance often work best when they're used hand-in-hand. Music that's too consonant may feel like it's lacking the spice and variety of dissonance; while music that's too dissonant may be not be particularly enjoyable or even annoying to listen to since the tension that is created is never properly resolved.

When successive sounds are considered, their consonance or dissonance depends in part on the ability of the listener to remember the first sound while the second sound (or pitch) is heard. This characteristic of the perception of consonance and dissonance is especially important for discussions of chords, harmony, and melody (more on this later).

Finally, while consonance and dissonance are often treated as a dichotomy, it is likely that they are instead opposite ends of a continuum. As a result, the term sonance is often used to describe the quality of an interval being described by the consonance-dissonance continuum.

Chapter 5: Scales

"The only truth is music."
— *Jack Kerouac*

Fundamentally, a musical scale is simply a collection of musical notes from which the notes in a piece of music might be chosen. Scales do not offer any guidance to the composer or musician as to what notes from the collection should be used. Neither do they suggest in what order the notes should be used or played. They don't even require that all of the notes in the scale are used and in fact allow other notes to be used (accidentals). Consequently, scales are only suggestive frameworks for music and not restrictive ones.

Moreover, the choice by a musician as to which scale to use is typically not be arbitrary. There are many possible scales in music, and each has a highly distinctive sound, though some are much more commonly used than others. Therefore, a composer or musician chooses to be guided in their work by a particular scale for purely creative reasons, e.g., to achieve a particular sound or set of sounds. Scales, like intervals, then are another critical building block in the creation of music.

In fact, the entire harmonic and melodic structure of a piece of music can often be determined or described in part with respect to scales. They are used to generate chords, build chord progressions, and create memorable melodies. They are also at the foundation of every symphony ever written, and a critical tool for every improvisational musician.

And so just as was the case with intervals, knowing scales not only conceptually, but also in practice, is critical to effectively composing and playing music.

Scales can contain five notes, seven notes, or many more. But all of them have some important things in common. They always are based on a central note or Root note. They also always have a characteristic interval formula consisting of tones (whole steps) and semitones (half-steps) between the notes. If you know the root note and the interval formula for a scale, you should be able to easily identify the notes contained in that scale.

The Chromatic Scale

The most fundamental scale in Western music is the Chromatic scale. In fact, it is so important that it is often referred to as the master scale. As discussed earlier, the chromatic scale contains the 12 notes present in every octave, broken up into 12 half step intervals. Selecting notes from this set of 12 and arranging them into patterns of semitones and whole tones creates other scales. In other words, all other scales are derived from the Chromatic scale.

The Chromatic scale itself is very rarely used as the basis for composing music, because there are just too many different possible notes and intervals to choose from and no structure or guidance for the composer and musicians as to what sounds good and what does not. The main significance of the Chromatic scale is as a starting point in that it defines the full set of notes from which all other scales are derived.

There are a few other basic types of scales, and understanding these types can make learning scales a lot easier. Common types of scales include the natural major, the natural minor, the harmonic minor, the melodic minor, and the pentatonic. Each of these types will be discussed in more detail in this chapter.

The Major Scale

The Major scale is one of the most commonly used musical scales, especially in Western music. It is often the first scale musicians learn about and all other scales are based on it or compared to it, often unfavorably. It is also particularly easy to recognize when you hear it. When played in sequence, the notes of the Major scale are the basis for the well-known do-re-mi-fa-so-la-ti-do "solfege" exercise. In fact, before it was turned into a song in The Sound of Music, this exercise was originally created as a memory pneumonic for teaching the notes of the Major scale.

It is also the scale from which songs like "Whistle While You Work," "Happy Birthday," and "Mary Had a Little Lamb" are composed. Moreover, several well known songs by the Beatles are also written in major scales, e.g., "Let It Be," "Imagine," and "While My Guitar Gently Weeps."

The Major scale is made up of seven (diatonic) notes and it always follow the interval pattern whole step, whole step, half step, whole step, whole step, whole step, and half step (WWHWWWH). The first note (and last) in the scale is of course the Root note (or tonic) and determines the name of the scale, e.g., C Major.

Each of the eight notes in a major scale also has a name:

1st note: Root/Tonic
2nd note: Supertonic
3rd note: Mediant
4th note: Subdominant
5th note: Dominant
6th note: Submediant
7th note: Leading tone (or leading note)
8th note: Root/Tonic

Each of these numbers associated with a note in the scale is also known a scale degree.

In terms of intervals, then, the Major scale consists of: A Root note (R), and then with the next note a whole step above that, the interval is a Major 2nd (M2) . This is followed by another note a whole step above that, so the interval in relation to C is a Major 3rd (M3). The next note is a half step above, and so the interval relative to C is a Perfect 4th (P4). Then a Perfect 5th (P5), a Major 6th (M6), and finally a Major 7th (M7). The distance between the 7th note and the first note of the next octave is of course also a half-step.

C Major. The simplest major scale to write is C Major, the only major scale not requiring sharps or flats. It uses only the notes C, D, E, F, G, A, B, and C, so it is then also a diatonic scale. Notice how this starting note and interval pattern perfectly corresponds with the white keys of the piano. This is a special property of the C Major scale. Other Major scales use the same seven note letters, but of course in a different order, and with sharp (#) and flat (b) symbols to preserve the Major scale pattern of intervals.

Other Major Scales. Since there are 12 notes in the Chromatic scale (octave), and each one can be the Root note for a Major scale, there are then twelve possible Major Scales. However, the construction of eleven of those scales is a bit more complicated than it is for the C Major scale. For example, assume we start with the Root note A#. As we move upward, the next note would be C. This is because in the Major scale interval pattern, the second note is always one whole step (one tone) or two semitones above the letter name of the Root note.

Similarly, then, the next note in the scale would be D, which is one full tone above C. And following the same standard pattern, the next note in the scale would be D#, because the scale pattern says that the next note up would be one half step (one semitone) above the D.

However, this creates a problem. There is another simple rule in the creation of scales that says that there cannot be two notes with the same letter name in the scale. A D followed by D# breaks this rule. Also, B is missing from the scale, and that breaks another rule: that all possible notes in the scale be represented. However, we can overcome both problems if we write the scale as: A#-B#-C##-D#-E#-F##-G##-A#. Notice that the appropriate interval pattern for a Major scale is maintained and all letter names are present but not duplicated.

But what exactly are C##, F##, and G##? Well, if you start at C, and move up two half steps, you end up at D. These notes would be pronounced as C double sharp, F double sharp, and G double sharp, respectively (in sheet music, the symbol x may be used instead of ##).

So while the rule says that the letter name D cannot appear in the scale more than once, if you represent the D note as C##, you can get around that limitation.

Double sharps and flats are rare but acceptable, and may often be necessary to preserve the correct interval pattern in the scale. Of course, if you play the notes of this scale on a piano, there is no such thing as a C## key. You would still play the D key.

We see something even similar if look at the notes of the G# Major scale: G♯, A♯, B♯, C♯, D♯, E♯, F##, and G#. The next to last note in this hypothetical scale is pronounced F double sharp. Of course, F## is just an enharmonic spelling of the natural note G.

As another example, consider the C# Major scale which is almost identical to the C Major scale, except that every note is sharp: C♯, D♯, E♯, F♯, G♯, A♯, B♯, and C#.

First, notice that it contains the notes E# and B#. How is that possible when there are no such keys on a piano keyboard? As already explained, writing out a scale often requires that alternative (enharmonic) spellings be used in order to be consistent with the rules. So E# is used simply as another name for F natural, and B# as another name for C natural.

For the C# Major scale, the letters F and C are used for the notes F# and C#, but the letters E and B are not present. So E# can used for the third note, B# can used for the seventh note, and everything then is consistent with the rules and fits together. Of course, if the scale intervals are written or played descending, C♭ can be used for B natural and F♭ can be used for E natural.

No matter what instrument you play, mastering scales is a worthwhile goal. If you are given a scale name, do you know how to play degrees 1-8 on your particular instrument? What if you are asked to play the sequence 5-3-2-1-6-4-5-8?

Learning to do this for each of the twelve Major scales, on your particular instrument, can be a worthwhile task and an important step in learning to play that instrument.

Figure 5.1: The Most Common Major Scales

Major scales with no sharp or flat:

C Major Scale: C, D, E, F, G, A, B, C

Major scales with sharps:

G Major Scale: G, A, B, C, D, E, F♯, G

D Major Scale: D, E, F♯, G, A, B, C♯, D

A Major Scale: A, B, C♯, D, E, F♯, G♯, A

E Major Scale: E, F♯, G♯, A, B, C♯, D♯, E

Major scales with flats:

F Major Scale: F, G, A, B♭, C, D, E, F

B Flat Major Scale: B♭, C, D, E♭, F, G, A, B♭

E Flat Major Scale: E♭, F, G, A♭, B♭, C, D, E♭

A Flat Major Scale: A♭, B♭, C, D♭, E♭, F, G, A♭

Enharmonic Major Scales – Same pitches but different note names

B Major Scale: B, C♯, D♯, E, F♯, G♯, A♯, B

C Flat Major Scale: C♭, D♭, E♭, F♭, G♭, A♭, B♭, C♭

F Sharp Major Scale: F♯, G♯, A♯, B, C♯, D♯, E♯, F♯

G Flat Major Scale: G♭, A♭, B♭, C♭, D♭, E♭, F, G♭

C Sharp Major Scale: C♯, D♯, E♯, F♯, G♯, A♯, B♯, C♯

D Flat Major Scale: D♭, E♭, F, G♭, A♭, B♭, C, D♭

The (Natural) Minor Scales

Contrary to a popular misconception, the word "minor" does not mean that minor scales are somehow less important than Major scales. In fact, minor scales are quite common in classical music, jazz, and other styles of music. Minor scales are, however, quite different and so also sound quite different.

Minor scales contain the same seven (eight) notes as Major scales, although in a different order. And, like the Major scales, the Root note of a minor scale can be any twelve possible notes, and so there are also twelve possible natural minor scales. But there are also two common variations of the natural minor scale called minor harmonic and minor melodic.

As was the case with Major scales, each of the eight notes in a minor scale also has a name.

1st note: Tonic
2nd note: Supertonic
3rd note: Minor mediant
4th note: Subdominant
5th note: Dominant
6th note: Minor submediant ☐
7th note: Subtonic
8th note: Tonic

However, it important to point out here that in the harmonic and melodic minor scales, the seventh degree is called the leading tone, and in the melodic minor scale, the sixth degree is called the submediant.

Minor scales also have a characteristic interval pattern, but one that is somewhat different when compared to that of Major scales.

T-T-ST-T-T-T-ST (major)

T-ST-T-T-ST-T-T (minor)

Thus, a minor scale consists of the following intervals in relation to the Root: Major 2nd, minor 3rd, Perfect 4th, Perfect 5th, minor 6th, and a minor 7th.

Notice that the interval between the 1st and 3rd notes of the major scale is now the interval between the 3rd and 5th notes of the minor scale. In other words, the note that was the Major 3rd relative to the Root note in the Major scale is now a Perfect 5th in the minor scale, and the note that was Perfect 4th in the Major scale is now a minor 6th in the minor scale.

These differences in the order of the notes and the interval pattern give the minor scale a significantly different sound and specifically, a much more emotional quality, when compared to the Major scale. Music composed in minor scales is often described as slow, sad, deep, dark, mysterious, solemn, or ominous. However, others argue that sad, dark or mysterious qualities are not the only option, and that it is possible to create music in a minor scale that is both energetic and with a brighter and more positive emotional quality.

Furthermore, composers and musicians do not always agree on the usefulness of the minor scales. Some argue that with minor scales it is more difficult to create melodies that are memorable. However, it may also be argued that, because of the possible variations, the minor scales can provide more flexibility for a composer.

One common natural minor scale is A minor: A: A, B, C, D, E, F, G, A. Another is C minor: C-D-Eb-F-G-Ab-Bb-C

Figure 5.2: The Most Common Natural minor Scales

minor scales with no sharp or flat:

A minor: A, B, C, D, E, F, G, A

minor scales ascending and descending:

A#/Bb minor: A#, B#, C#, D#, E#, F#, G#, A# / Bb, C, Db, Eb, F, Gb, Ab, Bb

B minor: B, C#, D, E, F#, G, A, B

C minor: C, D, Eb, F, G, A, Bb, C

C#/Db minor: C#, D#, E, F#, G#, A, B, C# / Db, Eb, Fb, Gb, Ab, B$_{bb}$, Cb, Db

D minor: D, E, F, G, A, Bb, C, D

D#/Eb minor: D#, E#, F#, G#, A#, B, C#, D# / Eb, F, Gb, Ab, Bb, Cb, Db, Eb

E minor: E, F#, G, A, B, C, D, E

F minor: F, G, Ab, Bb, C, Db, Eb, F

F#/Gb minor: F#, G#, A, B, C#, D, E, F# / Gb, Ab, Bbb, Cb, Db, Ebb, Fb, Gb

G minor: G, A, Bb, C, D, Eb, F, G

G#/Ab minor: G#, A#, B, C#, D#, E, F#, G# / Ab, Bb, Cb, Db, Eb, Fb, Gb, Ab

Some example of songs based on the natural minor scale include "Hotel California" by the Eagles, "Should've Said No" by Taylor Swift, and "New Man" by Ed Sheeran.

Minor Harmonic Scales

One important variation on the natural minor scale is the minor harmonic scale. For some composers, the natural minor scales were a less preferred option when compared to Major scales, because the whole step appearing just before the tonic did not produce the same obvious tension-resolution quality. In fact, they felt that it was as if the natural minor had no leading note or tonic at all. This was considered to be a significant tonal weakness or flaw with the natural minor scales.

So they decided to tweak the natural minor by raising the seventh note (degree) of the scale one half step, and thus the interval between degree 6 and 7 becomes one and a half steps. This, in effect, artificially created a tonic-resolution feel. This revised natural minor is then called the harmonic minor scale.

The raised seventh degree does provide a more powerful tension quality —our ears sense the root coming - and so there is a stronger sense of resolution once the tonic is reached. It has been suggested that this is because the closer a note is to the tonic the more listeners feel the tension-resolution effect.

Two examples of harmonic minor scales are: the A harmonic minor scale are: A, B, C, D, E, F, G#, A; and the C harmonic minor scale: C-D-Eb-F-G-Ab-B-C

In terms of intervals in relation to the Root: Major 2nd, minor 3rd, Perfect 4th, Perfect 5th, minor 6th, and Major 7th.

So the harmonic minor structure is this: whole, half, whole, whole, half, whole + half, half or: T S T T S TS S

Because the Harmonic minor scales opened up more compositional options for building chords and composing melodies, they are one of the most commonly used minor scales by composers. Knowing the harmonic minor scales is also an important step in being able to improvise music more effectively because they give you a broader, more delicate range of options from which to choose.

Some examples of songs based on the harmonic minor scale include "You Are The Sunshine of My Life" by Stevie Wonder, "Sweet Dreams" by the Eurythmics, "California Dreamin" by the Mamas and the Papas, and "Sultans of Swing" by Dire Straights.

Figure 5.3: The Most Common minor Harmonic Scales

A minor: A, B, C, D, E, F, G#, A

minor harmonic scales ascending and descending:
A#/Bb minor: A#, B# C#, D#, E#, F#, G##, A# / Bb, C, Db, Eb, F, Gb, A, Bb

B minor: B, C#, D, E, F#, G, A#, B

C minor: C, D, Eb, F, G, Ab, B, C

C#/Db minor: C#, D#, E, F#, G#, A, B#, C# / Db, Eb, Fb, Gb, Ab, Bbb, Cb, Db

D minor: D, E, F, G, A, Bb, C#, D

D#/Eb minor: D#, E#, F#, G#, A#, B, C##, D# / Eb, F, Gb, Ab, Bb, Cb, D, Eb

E minor: E, F#, G, A, B, C, D#, E

F minor: F, G, Ab, Bb, C, Db, E, F

F#/Gb minor: F#, G#, A, B, C#, D, E#, F# / Gb, Ab, Bbb, Cb, Db, Ebb, F, Gb

G minor: G, A, Bb, C, D, Eb, F#, G

G#/Ab minor: G#, A#, B, C#, D#, E, F##, G# / Ab, Bb, Cb, Db, Eb, Fb, G, Ab

Minor Melodic Scales

However, from the perspective of some composers, although presented with more options, the harmonic minor scale was still not ideal for writing melodies. The augmented interval between the sixth and seventh degrees was a problem because listeners could sense the artificial spacing and this sounded awkward.

So they made another change: they added another accidental to raise the sixth scale degree by a half-step, resulting in an interval pattern of only whole steps and half-steps. The result is the melodic minor scale. Some examples of music that are based on this scale include "When You Wish Upon A Star," as well as "I Just Called To Say I Love You" by Stevie Wonder, and "Yesterday" by The Beatles.

One example of this scale is the A melodic minor. The notes are A, B, C, D, E, F♯, G♯ and A. Another is the C melodic minor scale: C, D, Eb, F, G, A, B, C.

The formula for a melodic minor scale is whole step – half step – whole step – whole step – whole step – whole step – half step (W-H-W-W-W-W-H).

The intervals of the melodic minor scale are then: Root, a Major 2nd, a minor 3rd, a Perfect 4th, a Perfect 5th, a Major 6th and a Major 7th.

Sonically, the melodic minor is distinctive. In the first half of the ascending scale, A-B-C-D-E follows the pattern of tone-semitone-tone-tone, the same as the natural minor. However, the second half, E-F♯-G♯-A, is a tone-tone-semitone pattern, which is the same as the beginning of a major scale pattern. Therefore, the scale starts off sounding minor, and then switches to sounding major. This lends an interesting, conflicting quality to the scale and places it somewhere between a major and minor. It also gives it internal dissonance in the form of tritones, which as was discussed earlier, is the name for an interval formed by three whole tones. This tension and ambiguity in the melodic minor scale make it perfect for jazz and experimental music, though it is found in classical and popular music as well. One example is the famous "Carol of the Bells":

However, there is one additional important feature of the melodic minor scale. It is not the same ascending and descending. When descending, the sixth and seventh notes (degrees) are lowered back down to their natural forms. More specifically, when using or playing an ascending interval, you add sharps to the sixth and seventh degrees of the natural minor scale, but during parts of the same piece, if the interval is descending, you use or play the notes as if you were in the natural minor scale. In other words, the descending formula is the natural minor scale formula backwards.

Thus, the notes of the C melodic minor scale descending are: C, D, Eb, F, G, Ab, Bb, C (the C natural minor scale).

Figure 5.4: The Most Common minor Melodic Scales ascending and descending

A minor: A, B, C, D, E, F#, G#, A / A, G, F, E, D, C, B, A

A#/Bb minor: Bb, C, Db, Eb, F, G, A, Bb / Bb, A, Ab, F, Eb, Db, C, Bb

B minor: B, C#, D, E, F#, G#, A#, A, B / B, A, G, F#, E, D, C#, B

C minor: C, D, Eb, F, G, A, B, C / C, Bb, Ab, G, F, Eb, D, C

C#/Db minor: C#, D#, E, F#, G#, A#, B#, C# / C#, B, A, G#, F#, E, D#, C#

D minor: D, E, F, G, A, B, C#, D / D, C, Bb, A, G, F, E, D

D#/Eb minor: D#, E#, F#, G#, A#, C, D, D# / D#, C#, B, A#, G#, F#, F, D#

E minor: E, F#, G, A, B, C#, D#, E / E, D, C, B, A, G, F#, E

F minor: F, G, Ab, Bb, C, D, E, F / F, Eb, Db, C, Bb, Ab, G, F

F#/Gb minor: F#, G#, A, B, C#, D#, E#, F# / F#, E, D, C#, B, A, G#, F#

G minor: G, A, Bb, C, D, E, F#, G / G, F, Eb, D, C, Bb, A, G

G#/Ab minor: G#, A#, B, C#, D#, E#, F##, G# / G#, F#, E, D#, C#, B, A#, G#

<u>Relative and Parallel Scales</u>. Finally, it is important to note that Major and minor scales that contain the same notes but have different Root notes are said to be relative to one another, e.g., C major and a natural minor. However, Major and minor scales that contain different notes but share the same Root note are said to be parallel to one another, e.g., C major and C minor.

Together, the combination of the Major and various minor scales is an extraordinary system, complex enough to challenge the greatest musical minds, yet also simple enough (with only 12 divisions of the octave) to be accessible and sonically comprehensible to even novice composers and musicians.

Pentatonic Scales

Pentatonic (five tone) scales, as the name implies, contain only five notes. More specifically, they use only the five notes from the Major and minor scales that sound the best together (very little dissonance). So the pentatonic scale is an especially good place to start if you are just getting started as a composer because everything you create based on this scale tends to sound pretty good. However, eventually you may discover the value of dissonance and tension in music and then graduate to using the full Major and minor scales.

While pentatonic scales may have a variety of different note and interval patterns, there are two in particular—the minor pentatonic scale and the major pentatonic scale— that are used most often. They are called "major" and "minor" because, as mentioned above, they are derived from the full 7-note Major and minor scales. There are also other pentatonic scales, especially in non-western music, which are more rare but still sometimes useful. For example, Chinese scales used to compose traditional Chinese folk music is a pentatonic (5-note) scale. In Western music, however, pentatonic scales are often used in blues, rock music, country music, jazz, and bluegrass music.

Minor Pentatonic Scale. The minor pentatonic scale is made up from five notes derived from the natural minor scale: for instance, the A minor pentatonic scale (A, C, D, E and G).

Thus, the interval pattern for a minor pentatonic is: WH W W WH W or (Whole Step+Half Step, Whole Step, Whole Step, Whole Step+Half Step, and Whole Step). Notice that there are no semitones (half steps) in the pattern. This is one of the characteristics of pentatonic scales that give them such a unique sound.

The relevant intervals in the scale relative to the Root then are: a minor 3rd, a Perfect 4th, a Perfect 5th, and a minor 7th.

As will be discussed later in this book, this scale works especially well if you make it the root of a chord. In fact, when you play the minor pentatonic scale, you may notice that it sounds a bit bluesy. That is because this scale, with the addition of one note, e.g., D#, is also often referred to as the "blues scale," and the added note is often referred to as the "blue note."

In fact, the A minor pentatonic scale is probably the most-used scale used by guitarists who play rock music. Songs from bands like Pink Floyd, the Rolling Stones, Led Zeppelin, AC/DC, Aerosmith, Van Halen, Guns N' Roses, Nirvana, and Foo Fighters are all based in part on minor pentatonic scales. For example, Led Zeppelin's classic hit "Stairway To Heaven" uses the A minor pentatonic along with the A natural minor scales. The same is true of Adele's "Love In The Dark."

Here is a list of all twelve minor pentatonic scales:

 A minor pentatonic: A, C, D, E, G, A
 Bb minor pentatonic: Bb, Db, Eb, F, Ab, Bb
 B minor pentatonic: B, D, E, F#, A, B
 C minor pentatonic: C, Eb, F, G, Bb, C
 C# minor pentatonic: C#, E, F#, G#, B, C#
 D minor pentatonic: D, F, G, A, C, D
 Eb minor pentatonic: Eb, Gb, Ab, Bb, Db, Eb
 Em pentatonic: E, G, A, B, D, E
 F minor pentatonic: F, Ab, Bb, C, Eb, F
 F#m pentatonic: F#, A, B, C#, E, F#
 G minor pentatonic: G, Bb, C, D, F, G
 G# minor pentatonic: G#, B, C#, D#, F#, G#

Major Pentatonic Scale. The Major pentatonic scale, which is derived from the Major scale, is very different from minor pentatonic scale — because even though it consists of the same 5 notes — (C, D, E, G and A) —the notes are in a different order and so it also has a completely different interval pattern: W-W-WH-W-WH.

Thus, the five intervals of the Major pentatonic scale in relation to the root, are: a Major 3rd, a Perfect 4th, a Major 6th, and a Major 7th.

Like the minor pentatonic scale, the major pentatonic scale is simple and easily recognizable. In fact, it is the scale used for the hymn "Amazing Grace." Because of the different intervals pattern, this scale can have a lighter, more cheerful, and positive sound than a minor scale. It is derived from the Major scale, after all.

One example is called the G major pentatonic scale and it's also an important and very common scale in blues, country, rock, pop, etc. "Honky Tonk Woman" by The Rolling Stones, "Wish You Were Here" by Pink Floyd, and "Sweet Home Alabama" by

Lynyrd Skynyrd, are all based in part on the G major pentatonic scale. In contrast, "Maggie May" by Rod Stewart, is based on the D major pentatonic scale.

Here is a list of all twelve major pentatonic scales:

    C Major pentatonic: C, D, E, G, A, C
    C# Major pentatonic: C#, D#, E#, G#, A#, C#
    Db Major pentatonic: Db, Eb, F, Ab, Bb, Db
    D Major pentatonic: D, E, F#, A, B, D
    Eb Major pentatonic: Eb, F, G, Bb, C, Eb
    E Major pentatonic: E, F#, G#, B, C#, E
    F Major pentatonic: F, G, A, C, D, F
    F# Major pentatonic: F#, G#, A#, C#, D#, F#
    Gb Major pentatonic: Gb, Ab, Bb, Db, Eb, Gb
    G Major pentatonic: G, A, B, D, E, G
    Ab Major pentatonic: Ab, Bb, C, Eb, F, Ab
    A Major pentatonic: A, B, C#, E, F#, A
    Bb Major pentatonic: Bb, C, D, F, G, Bb
    B Major pentatonic: B, C#, D#, F#, G#, B

Chapter 6: Keys

"Music gives a soul to the universe, wings to the mind, flight to the imagination and life to everything."
— *Plato*

As discussed in the preceding chapter, any group of musical notes, e.g., an octave, can also be referred to as a scale. When musicians compose a piece of music, they typically do not use all of the possible notes available to them. They use only those notes in a predetermined scale or "palette" of notes. Usually, this is because those specific notes sound particularly well together and the musician prefers that particular sound.

The Tonic Note

When a musical composition is written using only the notes included in a particular scale, there is a tendency for one of those pitches or notes to become the tonal center of that music acoustically (listeners can hear it) . That tonal center is typically the Root note of the scale and is also called the tonic note. Such music is often described as tonal or as having tonality, and almost all music is tonal. In fact, both musicians and non-musicians have a natural sense of when music is tonal and when it is not. If a piece of music lacks a tonal center it is said to be "atonal" and usually doesn't sound especially good. It may leave the listener with a feeling of incompleteness or that the music is somehow not finished.

The tonic note "sounds" or "feels" like a "home" or resting place for the music using that scale, and is frequently repeated in the music, and returned to at the end of the music.

For example, "do" in the do-re-mi song, is the tonic for the scale on which the song is based, and as you may recall, it is returned to at the end of the singing of the scale, e.g., do-re-mi-fa-so-la-ti-do. Returning to the tonic note at the end of a piece of music is referred to as "resolution to tonic." That is because in such music, listeners often experience a sense of a starting point, followed by a sense of unresolved movement and tension, and followed finally by a sense of "resolution," as the music returns "home" to and finishes with the tonic note.

When music is said to be written in a particular key, fundamentally what is being said is that the music has a tonal quality.

However, keys are also given a name, e.g., C Major, and the name of a given key specifies two things: first, the tonal pitch (tonic) around which the key is organized, e.g., C, and second, what sort of scale is built atop that pitch, e.g., a Major. For example, music could be written in the key of "D major" or 'B flat minor" (or you can just say "in D", if it's a major key)

Music written in certain "keys", called "Major" keys, usually sounds bright, cheerful, happy, and positive. Music written in other keys, called "minor" keys, often sounds more ominous, sad, or mysterious.

The tonal quality of music can be achieved in a number of different ways: as a product of melodic implication, as a harmonic resolution, or via assertion.

Melodic Implication. When the melody of a piece of music clearly highlights the tonic note, or the tonic note becomes a point of rest and release for the melody, this is called melodic implication. More often than not, this is made explicitly clear when, at the end of a phrase or section of music, a melody will come to rest on its tonic pitch. This will be discussed in more detail in a later chapter.

Harmonic Resolution. Tonality can also be achieved via harmonic resolution. A harmony, or chord, is the simultaneous sounding of three or more different pitches, and the movement, or progression, from chord to chord constitutes a harmonic progression. The two most important notes in any diatonic scale are the tonic (the first) and dominant (the fifth) notes. By extension, the two most important chords in a harmonic progression are those built on the tonic and dominant pitches - tonic chord (symbolized as I) and dominant chord (symbolized as V). The tonic chord, in which the tonic pitch is the root of the chord, represents rest and resolution. The dominant chord in which the dominant pitch is the root of the chord, represents tension—unrest and irresolution. There is no more effective way to establish an irrefutable and powerful sense of resolution to tonic than to play the harmonic progression V–I in any given key. This will also discussed in more detail in a later chapter.

Assertion. Tonality via assertion is when a single note is sustained for so long and/or repeated so often that it becomes, by sheer commonality of its assertion, the obvious tonal center in a given section or piece of music.

Not all music features clear and unambiguous tonal centers. In fact, many early-and mid- 20th-century composers tried to avoid creating any sense of tonality whatsoever. However, the so-called atonal music that they produced is probably mischaracterized because true atonality is, in reality, almost impossible to achieve.

The concept of keys can often be especially confusing for beginners at learning music theory, in part because of inconsistencies in the use of terminology. When clearly discussing keys, some writers will refer to them as scales. As we will discuss in more detail in a later chapter, the palette of notes used for a key is indeed also a type of scale, or may be based on a scale, but it is not the only type of scale, and it is not the scale on which it is based. There are many types of musical scales that are used in other ways. In other words, a key is a scale, but not all scales are keys.

Another frequent source of confusion is inconsistency in discussing the number of notes that make up a particular key. Some writers will say seven, others eight, and others will say 12. Those that say seven or twelve are perhaps confusing the "key" with the scale on which it is based. The full octave scale corresponding to a particular key does indeed contain seven natural notes designated by the letters A, B, C, D, E, F, and G, and five sharp and flat notes, for a total of twelve notes. However, musical keys do not use all of the twelve notes of a given octave to build the palette of the key. The seven notes that are used are called the "diatonic" notes, whereas the five notes from the octave that are not used are called the "chromatic" notes. So while a scale does indeed contain twelve notes, it would be incorrect to say that a key based on it contains twelve notes.

Actually, a musical "key" technically contains eight notes, because the Tonic repeats at the end of the list of notes in the key, just at a pitch one full octave higher. But some writers leave it out when indicating the notes in a given key. In a later chapter of this book, we will discuss why it is important to include it, and so going forward we will always describe a key as containing eight notes.

The various possible keys available musicians to use in a composition can be represented in a diagram called the circle of fifths.

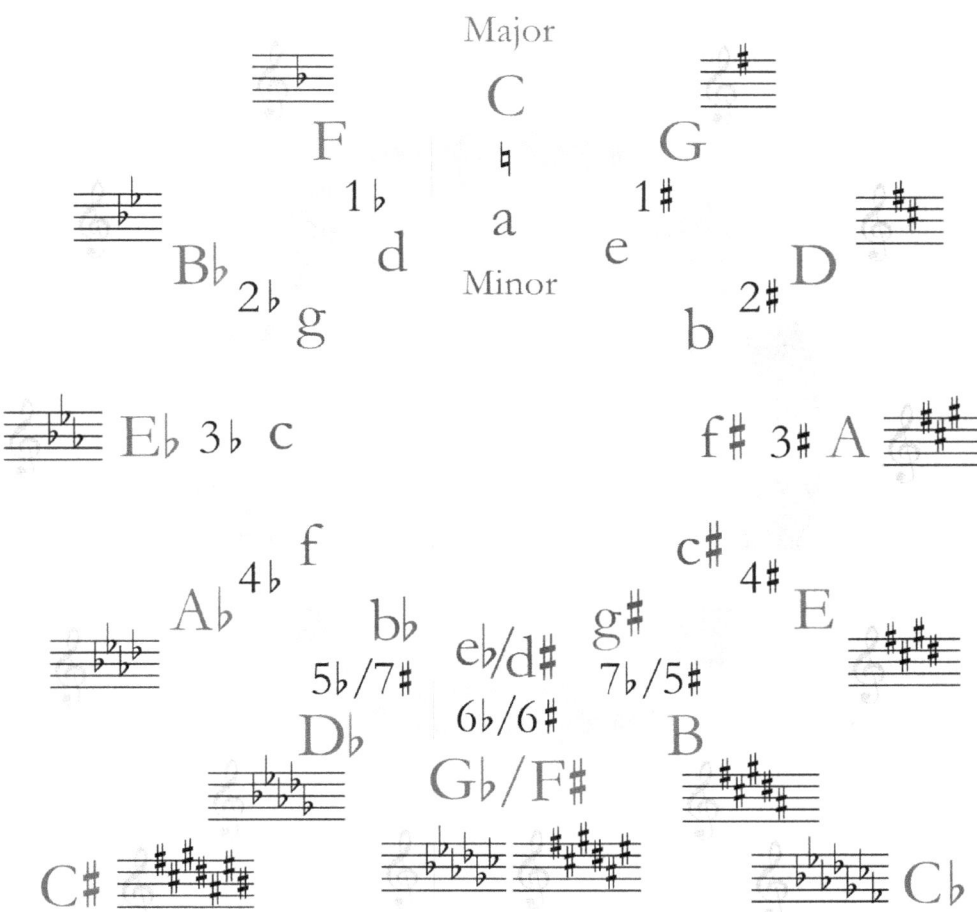

It is called The Circle of Fifths because each of the Major and Minor keys are separated by an equal distance: an interval of a perfect fifth (seven semitones). So, if you start at the top with the key of C Major/A Minor, and move clockwise adding an interval of a perfect fifth, you reach G Major/E minor.

The numbers inside the circle show the number of sharps or flats in the key signature, with the sharp keys going clockwise, and the flat keys counterclockwise from C major which has no sharps or flats. The circular arrangement also identifies enharmonic relationships in the circle, e.g., six sharps for the F♯ = G♭ Major keys and six flats for the D♯ = E♭ for minor keys. The major keys C♯ major or C♭ major are also indicated, and their positioning right next to D♭ major or B major is also significant. C♯ major or C♭ major can sometimes be more conveniently spelled as D♭ major or B major because they are also enharmonically equivalent.

Major Keys

Most Western music is written in one of the major keys. As discussed earlier, the key contains eight notes, with the eighth note duplicating the first (tonic) note one octave higher (double its frequency). But of course, these notes are different for each Major Key because the scale on which it is based starts on different notes.

Moreover, all major keys have the same pattern of intervals—half steps and whole steps—beginning with the note that names the key. That pattern is: whole step, whole step, half step, whole step, whole step, whole step, half step, and of course, it is the same pattern as that of the scale on which the key is based.

As the Circle of Fifths diagram shows, there are fifteen possible "major keys".

They are:

A major

A flat Major

B major

B flat major

C major

C flat major

C sharp major

D major

D flat major

E major

E flat major

F major

F sharp major

G major

G flat major

Twelve of the Major Keys correspond to each of the twelve notes in the full octave scale on which the key is based. The other three are enharmonic spellings of the same key depending in how the enharmonic sharp or flat they contain is named.

For example, both G^b Major and F$^\#$ Major keys use the exact same set of notes. However, G^b Major is spelled using flat note names (G^b, A^b, B^b, C^b, D^b, E^b, and F), while F$^\#$ Major is spelled with equivalent sharp note names (F$^\#$, G$^\#$, A$^\#$, B, C$^\#$, D$^\#$, and E$^\#$).

Prior to the adoption of the equal temperament tuning system, music composed in different Major keys sounded more less similar than it does now. The differences heard now are largely the result of differences in the timbre of notes when played on certain instruments or produced by different voices.

Minor Keys

Minor Keys contain the same notes as Major Keys. However, they differ from Major Keys in the order of these notes and so also how these notes are put together into unique patterns of intervals.

In contrast to the Major Keys, the minor Keys essentially use the same pattern of intervals only for the first five notes: 2-1-2-2-1. As discussed in the previous chapter, the sixth and seventh notes are frequently changed creating the harmonic and melodic variations on each of the natural Minor Keys. This provides for much more flexibility in minor keys, and the consequence of this is that there are many more possible minor Keys: 45 total.

As the Circle of Fifths diagram shows, there are fifteen natural minor keys. Twelve of them correspond to each of the twelve notes in the full octave scale on which the key is based. As was the case with Major Keys, the other three are enharmonic spellings of the same key depending on how the enharmonic sharps or flats they contain are named. Taking into account the variations possible because of the increased flexibility of minor Keys, here is a complete list of the possible minor Keys.

A minor natural

A minor harmonic

A minor melodic

A flat minor natural

A flat minor harmonic

A flat minor melodic major

A sharp minor natural

A sharp minor harmonic

A sharp minor melodic

B minor natural

B minor harmonic

B minor melodic

B flat minor natural

B flat minor harmonic

B flat minor melodic

C minor natural

C minor harmonic

C minor melodic

C sharp minor natural

C sharp minor harmonic

C sharp minor melodic

D minor natural

D minor harmonic

D minor melodic

D sharp minor natural

D sharp minor harmonic

D sharp minor melodic

E minor natural

E minor harmonic

E minor melodic

E flat minor natural

E flat minor harmonic

E flat minor melodic

F minor natural

F minor harmonic

F minor melodic

F sharp minor natural

F sharp minor harmonic

F sharp minor melodic

G minor natural

G minor harmonic

G minor melodic

G sharp minor natural

G sharp harmonic

G sharp melodic

Relative and Parallel Keys

Any given key has three other keys that are considered as being closely related to it. They are the two like keys that lie on either side of the given key in the circle of fifths and the given key's relative Major or minor. Taking C Major as an example, the two like keys are the two Major keys on either side of C Major in the circle of fifths. They are G Major to the right (sharp side) and F Major to the left (flat side).

Major and minor keys that share key signatures are called relative keys. For example, A minor is the relative minor of C major; C major is the relative major of A minor. Relative major and minor keys are those that share the same pitches but have a different tonic, and so sound completely different.

In contrast, parallel major and minor keys are those that share the same tonic but have different key signatures. The keys of C major and C minor are an example of parallel major and minor keys. They most certainly will also sound quite different.

There are many possible keys, and the vast majority of music ever written uses at least one of these possible keys. Since a key contains only a limited number of possible notes, that can make music composition a much less complicated task. It can also be very useful information for musicians to know the key of a piece of music, especially those who improvise the music they play. It tells them what small subset of possible notes will sound good together. Any other notes can usually be ignored.

Key Signatures

In common music notation, it is often necessary to indicate what "key" is being used in a particular musical composition. This is done by including a "key signature" on the music staff right next to and just after the clef.

Figure 6.1: The Key Signature

A key signature is not the same as a key; key signatures are merely notational devices. It contains several useful pieces of information regarding the music that follows. First, the key signature tells the musician what scale the music is based on.

It also indicates how many sharp or flat notes are used in the composition, and more importantly, what they are. For example, as Figure 6.1 shows, E major contains four sharps and B major contains five sharps. Since each key contains a unique collection or pattern of sharps and flats, the key signature then also indirectly indicates the "key" of the composition.

This is because one can identify the specific "key" (and type) by carefully studying the unique configuration (where they are and what they are) of the sharps and flats for the key signature on the staff.

Taken together, the clef tells you the letter name of the note (A, B, C, etc.), and the key signature tells you whether the note is sharp, flat or natural. More specifically, when a sharp (or flat) appears on a line or space in the key signature, all the notes on that line or space, throughout the entire composition, are read (and played) as sharp (or flat), and all other notes with the same letter name in other octaves will also be sharp (or flat). For example, a sharp symbol on the top line of the treble staff applies to not only all F notes on that line, but all F notes throughout the entire composition, no matter where they appear on the staff. And if there are no flats or sharps listed after the clef symbol, then the key signature can be read as "all notes are natural" (C major).

Moreover, in all key signatures, the sharps or flats always appear in the same order from left to right. If a key signature contains only one sharp, it will always be an F sharp, so in any key signature F sharp will always be the first sharp listed. When a key signature contains two sharps, the sharps will always be F sharp and C sharp, so C sharp is always written, from left to right, as the second sharp in the key signature, and so on.

The standard order for sharps in any key signature is: F sharp, C sharp, G sharp, D sharp, A sharp, E sharp, B sharp.

In contrast, the standard order for flats in any key signature is the reverse order: B flat, E flat, A flat, D flat, G flat, C flat, F flat.

Thus, keys with only one flat (F major and D minor) will have a B flat; the keys with two flats (B flat major and G minor) will contain B flat and E flat; and so on.

If a piece of music (or part of a piece of music) is in a major key, then the notes in the corresponding major scale are considered diatonic notes, even if they are sharps or flats, and the notes outside the major scale are considered chromatic notes. For example, if the key of a piece of music is based the E♭ Major scale, then the seven pitches in the E♭ major key (E♭, F, G, A♭, B♭, C and D) are considered diatonic pitches, and the other five pitches (E♮, F♯/G♭, A♮, B♮, and C♯/D♭) are considered chromatic pitches. In this case, the key signature will have three flats (B♭, E♭, and A♭).

What Key Is It?

If you do not know the name of the key for a piece of music, the first place to look is the key signature. If you already know it is a Major Key, and the key contains sharps, the name of the key is one half step higher than the last sharp in the key signature. If the key contains flats, the name of the key signature is the name of the second-to-last flat in the key signature.

The only major keys that these rules do not work for are C major (no flats or sharps) and F major (one flat). It is easiest just to memorize the key signatures for these two very common keys.

Of course, you can also determine the Major Key of a piece of music by just comparing the key signature to those listed on the Circle of Fifths Diagram.

Unfortunately, this oversimplifies things a bit. What if you don't know if it is a major or minor key? One problem is that, as noted earlier, different major and minor keys may share the same key signature (enharmonic spelling). For example, G Major and E Minor are "relative keys" and so share a key signature of one sharp. Similarly, C major and A minor share the same key signature with no sharps or flats. You can easily determine the relative minor keys for any major key. It is always found three semitones down from the Major key. For example, the relative minor of C major is A minor. And, of course, on the Circle of Fifths diagram it is the key just inside the circle and next to C major.

Most music is written in major keys, so most of the time you can just assume that it is a major key. Another approach would be to try to identify the tonic, which likely will be the final note in the music, and/or a common note in the music. That should then help you determine major or minor, because even when relative keys have the same key signature, they will have different tonics.

Finally, it is also important to keep in mind that as the music progresses, the key of the music may change, usually after a double-bar or other obvious transition point. It is typically done to change up the feel of the song or to rekindle the interest of the listener. This is referred to as a "key change" or modulation. Often, this change will be indicated by the inclusion of a new key signature indicating the new key for the music going forward.

If the new key signature will have no sharps or flats, the new signature may contain natural note symbols in place of previous flat and sharp symbols so as to in effect cancel the previous signature. If the new signature occurs at the beginning of a new line on the page, the old signature may be repeated at the end of the previous line in order to make the change more noticeable.

Accidentals

For some musical compositions, only a few of the instances of a particular note are going to be played as a sharp (or flat). This is especially true when they are chromatic notes that are not part of the key in which the music is written. So they are in effect exceptions to the key signature. For example, when a scale on which a key is based has been augmented by adding additional natural, sharp, double sharp, flat, or double flat notes, the key signature is not changed and remains the appropriate signature corresponding to the unaltered scale and key. This is called chromatic alteration.

Similarly, when a minor harmonic or minor melodic key is used, both of which include notes that are not in the key signature—the notes that have altered relative to the natural minor.

In such cases, the special notes are marked individually on the staff with a sharp (or flat) sign right next to and in front of them. Such special instances of sharps and flats are called accidentals.

Figure 6.2: Accidentals

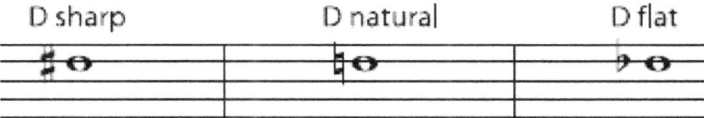

Transposition

An entire piece of music may be transposed from one key to another key for various purposes. For example, it may be done to accommodate the vocal range of a particular vocalist. If the vocalist has difficulty singing especially high notes or generating appropriate vocal power on such notes, the music may be modified or essentially rewritten in a different key. e.g. one with lower pitched notes. A similar thing might be done for a vocalist that has difficulty with low notes. Such transposition will raise or lower the overall pitch range, but preserve the interval relationships of the original key. For example, a transposition from the key C Major to the key D Major would raise all pitches of the piece of music by a whole step. Since the interval relationships remain unchanged, the transposition may not be noticeable to a listener. Music can be transposed from one Major key into another Major key, or from a minor key into another minor key. However, transposition is not always possible without substantially changing the sound of the music. Transposing music from a Major key into a minor key is extremely difficult and usually does not work out very well.

Chapter 7: Music and Time

"The most exciting rhythms seem unexpected and complex, the most beautiful melodies simple and inevitable."
— *W.H. Auden.*

Unlike static works of art such as a paintings, photographs, or sculptures, which exist as "all of what they are" at every moment in time from the point at which they are created, music is an art form in which the passage of time is an important element of the work. In other words, music does not just stand still. Instead, it moves forward, progresses, changes, evolves, develops, repeats, grows, declines, and eventually ends. Thus, music not just acoustic, it is also temporal.

But of course, music is not a continuous stream of noise. Rather, music is an art form made up of a series of distinct events that happen over a period of time, usually in creatively planned patterns, one after the other, like words in a sentence, sentences in a poem or story, or scenes in a movie. Moreover, with regard to music, the precise timing of the events is also especially important. Musical events must happen at precisely the right times, for precisely the right duration, and in precisely the right way, for the music to work.

Finally, just as is the case with language, comprehending what is being communicated in music is not just based on understanding a particular note or phrase, but rather how the notes and phrases fit together over time and gradually create the meaning.

It is the temporal qualities of music that will be the focus of this chapter. Future chapters will focus on topics such as chords and chord progressions, melodies, dynamics, and composition, all of which necessarily involve events happening over time, and so having some basic understanding of the temporal aspects of music will be essential for developing an understanding of those topics.

Temporal Qualities of Music

We can discuss the temporal qualities of music in terms of four fundamental elements, Beat, Tempo, Meter, and Rhythm.

1. **Beat**—the background pulse of a piece of music.

2. **Tempo**—the relatively fast or slow speed at which the music moves forward.

3. **Meter**—how beats are organized, along with accents, silence, and notes, into discrete segments in a piece of music.

4. **Rhythm**—the overall musical patterns established by the beat, tempo, and meter, and notes, along with the qualities of uniqueness, repetitiveness, expectancy, movement, and development.

Beat. On a fundamental level, music moves forward through time as a series of discrete pulses. By discrete, I mean that each pulse gives way to complete silence before the next pulse occurs. With regard to music, we often call our subjective experience of one of these pulses "a beat" (even though, technically, a single pulse may extend over more than a single beat). For example, if you tap your finger on a table four times, one right after the other, you have performed four beats. Notice that each tap was a distinct event, and not a continuous one.

Most importantly, it is a single "beat" that serves as the most basic organizing element for all music. Each tap on a drum, each note played (or vocalized) by a musician, or each silence, may count as one beat, with each piece of music made up of thousands of such beats occurring in succession.

Accents. In any series of beats, one or more of them may receive more emphasis or accent than others. In fact, the strongest or accented beat is usually the one that occurs just after the bar line. So, if while tapping your finger four times, you say "ONE-two-three-four, ONE-two-three-four, you are putting accent on the ONE beat. The ONE beat is then the strong beat, and the next three beats are weaker beats. Of course, the pattern could also have been one-TWO-three-FOUR, one-TWO-three-FOUR, or ONE-two-three, ONE-two-three.

In all of these cases, the accent was "vocal," but in composing music there are many possible ways of creating the desired emphasis on a beat, e.g., tapping a drum harder on the accented beat, using a different drum on the accented beat, playing or singing a note louder, playing or singing a note longer, playing a note with more intensity, playing or singing a note at a higher pitch, changing timbre on the accented note, etc. Any of these methods, when used correctly, can create emphasis that can be heard by listeners.

In any event, it is the number and relative positions of accented and unaccented beats that forms the "beat pattern" of a piece of music and underlies discussion of both meter and rhythm (more on this later).

Finally, as discussed earlier, music is not written on a staff in one long continuous stream. In order to keep music organized, and provide common reference points, written music is divided up into smaller chunks called measures or bars. Most important for the topics covered in this chapter is that each measure can contain only a limited and specific number of beats.

The Upbeat and Downbeat. The music concepts of beat and beat-pattern have evolved from centuries of study of human dance as well as from discussions of rhythmic patterns in poetry. When you place your foot down to begin a dance step, that is a strong first beat. As mentioned earlier, it is the first beat of a measure that usually receives the strongest accent and in fact this beat is called the Downbeat (crusis). In contrast, the Upbeat (anacrusis) is the last beat in the previous measure which immediately precedes the Downbeat.

Conductors communicate beat patterns with their baton in order to lead an orchestra or choir. The first beat of the measure is gestured with a downward motion, and in fact it is the reason why the first beat is called the Downbeat. Metaphorically, this is like putting the foot down on the first beat of a dance. Obviously, then the hand is raised to indicate an Upbeat.

This One Beat Up-One Beat Down relationship is a critical factor, both in terms of the composition of music and the subjective experience of music by listeners. It is the basis for the sense of forward movement in music. The Upbeat is an anticipation, a beginning, a request, a question, an opening. The Upbeat leads to the Downbeat and serves as a preparation for the Downbeat. On the other hand, the Downbeat is an ending, a fulfillment, a question answered, a promise kept, a completion; and this propels the music forward, so what happens on that beat needs to be clear, strong, powerful, attention getting, and should stand-out.

<u>Notes</u>. As discussed in Chapter 3, musical notes do not only tell you what pitch to play. By virtue of how they look, they also include information about how long (the duration) they should be played by an instrument or sung by a voice. So obviously, it is important for musicians to not only play (or sing) the right pitch, but also do so for the correct amount of time.

In any measure, a musician may play or sing four quarter notes in succession, one per beat, or play or sing two half notes, each lasting two beats, or they may play a whole note lasting for all four of the beats in a measure.

When there are four beats per measure, this is called Common Time, but other patterns are also possible (more on that later). The important point here is that, in Common Time, no matter what is done on each beat, the total number of beats per measure must always equal four.

Of course, as we already know, there are also musical notes that have shorter durational values than quarter notes: eighth notes, sixteenth notes, and even thirty-second notes and sixty-fourth notes. In Common Time, these notes would represent half-beats, quarter-beats, sixteenth beats, and thirty-second beats, respectively.

Musicians may also sometimes use dotted or augmented notes. The standard notation for this is to put a small dot next to the right side of the note. For example, a half note with a dot next to it says to play and hold the note for half again as many beats as the value of the note, e.g. three beats in the case of an augmented half note.

Triplets are another very common practice in music: three equal notes are being played in the space of two notes. The most common example is the 8th note triplet. An eighth note triplet is 3 eighth notes played in the space of 2 eighth notes (or one quarter-note); a quarter-note triplet spans the length of a half-note, and so on. So we also need a symbol that will allow us to communicate a length of one third (33.3%) of the specific note, e.g. the eighth note. This is done by grouping the three eighth notes with a beam (replacing the flags on each note), and then adding a '3' (or triplet) sign just above the beam. In fact, such beams are used only to group notes together that share a beat, never across beats.

Figure 7.1. Triplets on Musical Staff

Syncopation, which is common in dance music and a lot of popular music, occurs when a strong note is sounded either on a weak beat or off the beat, or when the sounding of a note is extended or suspended across multiple beats, or even across measure bars.

Rests. In music, the spaces between musical notes and phrases are often as important as the notes themselves. At the very least, these pauses allow the listener to absorb each musical note or phrase before the next one starts. In fact, music can be perceived by listeners as more satisfying if it has a good balance between musical activity and silence.

In music terminology, these silences are called rests. Rests also count as beats, so, for example, a musical measure might contain three notes and a rest (four beats total).

Similar to notes, there are whole rests, half rests, quarter rests, and so on. And there are symbols for each that are placed on the musical staff as instructions to the musician to be quiet for some period of time, or, in piano music, that the left or right hand should to stop playing for some period of time. Since there is to be no sound, the only information communicated by the rest symbol is the duration of the silence.

Figure 7.2. Rests on Musical Staff

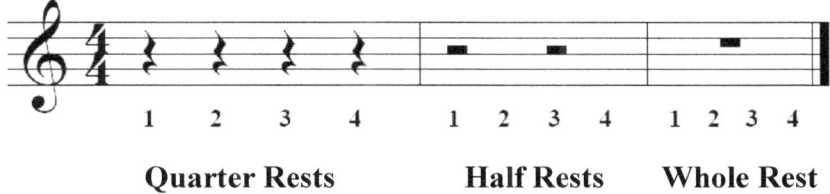

Normally rest symbols are placed in the same way as note symbols, evenly spaced across the bar from left to right.

Quarter rests and half rests can of course be mixed together with note symbols in any measure. However, the whole rest always fills an entire measure and so when it is used there can be no other notes or rests in that measure. In fact, while the whole-rest technically has a theoretical length of four quarter-notes, it is not uncommon for it to be used for a full measure regardless of how many beats are in that measure. In fact, it may be better to think of the whole rest symbol as indicating "rest for the whole measure".

Since it occupies the whole measure, the whole-rest symbol is always placed in the centre. The half-rest symbol looks similar to the whole-rest symbol, but it is placed above the third staff line, rather than hanging from the fourth line.

The eighth-rest, sixteenth-rest, thirty-second-rest and sixty-fourth-rest symbols use the same basic figure, but each has an extra hook. Notice that this parallels the way equivalent note symbols are constructed, with each having an extra flag. Two or more rest symbols together simply extends the size of the rest to their total length. Rests are also sometimes dotted or augmented, with the same implications as for augmented notes. And in common time, no matter how many different kinds of notes or rests are in a measure, the total number of beats in that measure must still always total to four.

Finally, it is important to point out that rests do not imply that the musician should let their mind wander while they are happening, even though for instrumentalists or singers in a group, the rests can often be quite long. Continuing to follow along with "the beat" of the music is essential if the musician is going to resume playing or singing at precisely the right beat or moment. Timing is everything in music. It is a good idea to become so familiar with the beat pattern of the music that you don't even realize you're counting beats anymore.

Tempo. The word tempo comes from tempus, the Latin word for time, and tempo is another crucial element in music. It describes the speed at which the beats happen — faster or slower.

The ticking of a clock and a human heartbeat are good examples of tempos. In the case of the clock, each individual "tick" is the equivalent of one beat and roughly corresponds to one second of time. So, for most clocks the tempo would be sixty ticks or beats per minute because there are sixty seconds per minute. Similarly, the normal resting heart rate or tempo for adult humans is between 60 to 100 beats per minute.

In fact, in music, tempo is also usually expressed in beats per minute, or BPM (for example 80 bpm means 80 beats per minute).

However, tempo is not only about the speed of the music. The tempo also is an important factor in setting the basic mood of a piece of music. Music that is played very, very slowly can impart a feeling of extreme somberness, whereas music played very, very quickly can seem happy and bright.

Of course, if a composer intends that a piece of music will be played quickly and cheerfully, or slowly and somberly, they need a way to communicate that intent to musicians. Prior to the 17th century, though, composers had no real control over how their transcribed music would be performed by others, especially by those who had never heard the pieces performed by their creator. It was only in the 1600s that the concept of using dynamic markings in sheet music began to be employed. Dynamic markings are like musical punctuation — they're the markings in a musical sentence that tell musicians how to most effectively convey the intent of the composer.

Tempo markings, which are only one of several types of dynamic markings, indicate how fast or slow music should be played. Traditionally, Italian words are used, simply because when these phrases came into use (1600–1750), the bulk of European music came from Italian composers. The markings are usually written above the staff near the clef symbol at the beginning of a piece of music.

Figure 7.3: The Most Common Tempo Markings

Larghissimo	Very, Very Slow
Grave	Very Slow
Lento	Slowly
Andante	At Walking Pace
Marcia Moderato	Moderately as in Marching
Moderato	Moderate Speed
Allegretto	Moderately Fast
Allegro	Fast

Allegrissimo	Very Fast
Presto	Very, Very Fast

These terms can be somewhat ambiguous, overlapping, and subject to interpretation, and so have had slightly different meanings at different points in history. For more precise indications of tempo, composers can also place a metronome mark in the music. The metronome is a mechanical or electronic device which can be set to click or flash a specified number of times per minute. For example, the metronome mark, ♩ = 80, would indicate that the piece should be played at the tempo of 80 beats per minute.

Figure 7.4. Metronome Mark on Musical Staff

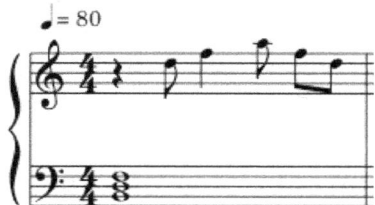

It should also be noted that tempo can change during a piece of music. Classical music routinely uses tempo changes to add expression and drama. For example, it is not uncommon to use a gradual slowdown in the last few bars of a song (called rallentando) to produce a more satisfying ending. Less common is the opposite effect - accelerando - where the tempo gradually increases. You will sometimes hear accelerando in dance or folk songs - such as Zorba The Greek - as they pick up speed. The following tempo markings indicate that the tempo should change:

Figure 7.5: Common Tempo Change Markings

Accelerando	Getting Faster
Ritardondo	Getting Slower
Rallentando	Gradually Slowing Down
A Tempo	Return to Original Pace

Meter. In any given piece of music, the pattern of strong and weak beats, the presence of inaudible but implied rest beats, the grouping of beats, and rests into measures, and the tempo, combine to give each piece of music complex and distinctive temporal characteristics. So does the varying durations of notes, and their articulation (more on this later). We call these temporal characteristics the meter of a piece of music.

Western music inherited the concept of meter from lyric poetry where it can denotes the number of lines in a verse; the number of syllables in each line; and the arrangement of those syllables as long or short, accented or unaccented. Haiku poetry is a very good example of this, as are limericks,

If you tap your finger on a table, then wait approximately one second, then tap again, and then again wait one second, you have not only performed four beats, but also beats with a specific pattern. Of course, other beat patterns are possible: for example, tap, pause, pause, pause, or tap, tap, pause, pause. Although different, each of these examples also contains four beats (some accented and some not accented). These patterns and how quickly they progress, are then key elements in the meter. You may also be familiar with the 'one - two - three - one - two - three' feel of a waltz, or the 'left - right - left - right' feel of a march. These are both also examples of meter.

Rhythm. There is much disagreement amongst music theorists as to what constitutes rhythm, and there are many reasons for this. In part, it is because rhythm has often been confused with one or more of its constituent, but not wholly separate, elements, such as beat, accent, meter, and tempo. This confusion can be exacerbated by the use of the term, often by the same writer in the same work, to refer to very different aspects of music, e.g., a pattern of beats and the pattern of notes of differing durations. Another compounding factor is that various types of instruments: drums, wood blocks, bass, bass guitar, piano, and even synthesizers may all be considered rhythm instruments, depending on the context. It may also be then that rhythm occurs on many different levels in music and so for any clear definition, those layers need to be teased apart. Finally, there is also clearly a subjective component to rhythm, and this often gets confused with the objective characteristics of the music.

On a very basic and objective level, rhythm certainly refers to the repetition in patterns of beats, silence (rests), and emphasis (accents) in music. It may even be argued that music requires rhythm. In fact, for some types of music, the rhythm is and is intended to be the most important component of the music. This is certainly true of drum solos. Rhythmic chants also fit this description. Also, music composed primarily for dancing, e.g., some music by Michael Jackson, and modern electro pop and trance music (Infernal's From Paris To Berlin), is primarily rhythmic, with the actual notes being played or lyrics of less importance. Similarly, in hip hop music, the rhythmic delivery of the lyrics is the most important element of the style.

However, rhythm can also obviously function as the propulsive engine of a piece of music because it gives a foundation to a composition and provides guidance for musicians playing that music. Most musical ensembles, like symphony orchestras, big bands, marching bands, and folk, pop, and rock groups, contain a "rhythm section" that is responsible for providing the rhythmic backbone for the music of the entire group.

Another element of music that often gets discussed in relation to rhythm is the creative and progressing pattern of notes of varying durations, played by one or more instruments, along with rests of varying durations, in a piece of music. As I will discuss later, this is essentially what constitutes the melody of a piece of music. And while there clearly can be rhythm without melody, when there is a clearly defined melody, aspects of that melody can also be experienced by listeners as contributing to the overall rhythm of the music, above and beyond what is contributed by a rhythm section.

Finally, rhythm is also, at least in part, subjective. It involves our initial perceptions of variations as well as pattern recognition (which some people are better at than others); specifically, the recognition and anticipation of a pattern of beats, some accented and some not, that we mentally abstract from the music as it unfolds in time. And we don't always see the patterns immediately. But when we do recognize the patterns, we then develop expectations regarding what will happen next. In fact, once we recognize the pattern, we often react behaviorally to our perceptions of the rhythm: we tap our feet, we dance, we march, because we "feel" the rhythm internally.

Moreover, in everyday colloquial talk, when we say of someone that they are "keeping time" or "in time" with the music, what we are saying is that they are demonstrating the ability to perceive, comprehend, and consistently replicate in their own behavior, e.g. hand clapping, foot tapping, drumming, etc., the unique rhythmic pattern of the music they are hearing.

When we say that someone has "rhythm" what we are in effect saying is that the person has perhaps a better than average ability or even a special ability to hear, sense, recognize, understand, feel, and replicate precisely the rhythmic qualities of music. This ability is indeed one quality that distinguishes great musicians from not so great ones. Drummers certainly rely on their abilities to comprehend and reproduce in a consistent way the rhythm underlying a piece of music. Pianists rely on their sense of rhythm to keep the pace of their playing consistent throughout a performance, and marching bands coordinate their music with their movement, as well as with each other, because of their sensitivity to the rhythm.

It may also be rhythm should not be understood as simply a series of discrete independent units, e.g., beats, notes, accents, etc., strung together in a mechanical, additive, way like beads. Instead, it might be better to think of rhythm as an organic process of understanding in which smaller temporal elements add up synergistically over time, evolving into a experience that is greater than the sum of its parts—an experience that we eventually come to recognize and define as the rhythm of the music.

Time Signatures

In written musical notation, there is a common method for communicating to musicians the particular meter of a piece of music. It is done with a Time Signature.

Figure 7.6. Time Signature on Musical Staff

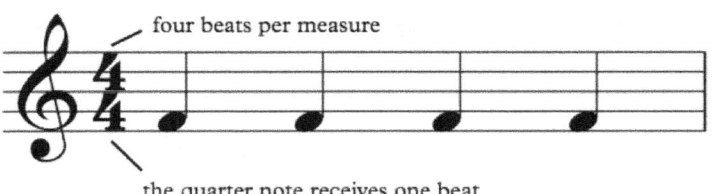

Along with Key Signatures, Time signatures are one of the most important forms of musical notation. Time signatures consist of two numbers, resembling a fraction (but they should not be confused with fractions). The time signature is always placed on the musical staff to the right of the clef symbol, just below tempo notations, and just after the key signature. And strictly speaking, the numbers should be placed one on top of the other, as they appear on staff lines.

The time signature says two things: how many beats are in a measure, and which value of written note is to be counted as a single beat.

If the top number is three, then each measure contains three beats. If the top number is four, then each measure contains four beats.

If the bottom number is four, then the largest note that can occupy one beat is a quarter note (two eighth notes, four sixteenth notes, etc., could also occupy one beat). Moreover, four is not the only number which can appear on the bottom of a time signature. For example, instead of quarter-notes, time signatures can also use an eighth-note as the maximum size of one beat. This is quite common. Other maximum beat sizes, such as whole-notes, half notes, sixteenth-notes, thirty-second-notes, and so on, are also theoretically possible, but are not particularly useful and are generally quite rare.

Another important point here is that the time signature in effect also determines the actual length of the measure. For example, when the bottom number is four, and the top number is four, the measure must be the equivalent of four quarter notes long. But any combination of notes or rests could be used to fill this space, e.g., one whole note, one whole rest, two half notes, one half note and a half rest, three quarter notes and a quarter rest, two quarter notes and a half rest, three quarter notes and two eighth notes, two quarter notes, one eighth note, and two sixteenth notes, etc. As long as the total value of the symbols included in the measure total up to no more than the length of four quarter notes, consistency with the time signature has been maintained.

But what if the bottom number is two and the top number three? This means that there are three beats in the measure, and each beat will be a half-note. Thus, the measure is three half notes long, and this also could be manifested in numerous ways, e.g., a whole note followed by a half note, a whole rest, or a single dotted whole note.

Common Time

As mentioned earlier, common time uses the 4/4 time signature, which indicates a four beat measure, where each beat is a quarter-note long. This is by far the most used time signature used by composers and you will often see it notated simply as a 'C' for common time.

The two basic beat patterns or meters in music are duple and triple. An example of duple meter is a march, where the LEFT – right – LEFT – right, is best represented by STRONG – weak, STRONG – weak. An example of triple meter is a typical waltz, ONE – two – three, ONE – two – three.

Types of Time Signatures

Time signatures can be sorted into different types along two dimensions as the table below indicates.

The first dimension is simple or compound time. The second dimension is duple, triple, or quadruple time.

Figure 7.7. Time Signatures

	Simple Time	Compound Time
Duple Time	2/2, 2/4, 2/8	6/8, 6/4
Triple Time	3/4, 3/2, 3/8	9/8, 9/2, 9/4
Quadruple Time	4/4, 4/2, 4/8	12/8, 12/16

Simple Time

Simple Duple. For example, 2/4 time is Simple Duple time. Duple refers to the two beats per measure (the top number), whereas Simple, based on the bottom number, means that each beat can be divided up into two notes. Other examples of simple duple time would include: 2/8, and 2/2, also known as "cut time" (or alla breve). The 2/2 time signature is also alternatively represented by a C symbol except that the C has a slash through it—the C of Common Time is being slashed or "cut."

Simple Triple. An example would be 3/4 time. Triple refers to three beats per measure (top number), even though the bottom number still indicates that each beat can be divided into two notes. So a 3/4 time signature indicates a Triple (three-beat) meter, where each beat is a quarter-note long. The total length of each bar will therefore be three quarter-notes, or 3/4 of a whole-note. Similarly, 3/2 and 3/8 are simple triples.

Simple Quadruple. This would include 4/4 (common) time as well as 4/2 time and 4/8 time. There are four beats per measure, but depending on the bottom number, those four beats may be composed of one quarter note each, two eighth notes each, or covering two half notes.

A simple meter time signature will always have 2, 3, or 4 as the top number, and any time you are tempted to count "one two one two" you are dealing with simple time.

Compound Time

Compound time is the name given to music when the beats can be divided into thirds. Whenever you count to a piece "one two three one two three", as for a waltz, you are counting to compound time.

Compound Duple. An example of a compound duple would be 6/8 time. Notice that the six eighth notes can be grouped in either of two ways using beams: as two beats made up of three eighth notes each, or as three beats of two eighth notes each. However, since the latter pattern is exactly the same as the 3/4 Simple Triple time, the 6/8 meter is always classified as a compound duple.

In any compound meter, the beat unit is always a dotted note. Also, any time signature with a 6 on top will be a Compound Duple, e.g., 6/8 or 6/4.

Compound Triple. An example of a Compound Triple would be 9/8. There are nine beats composed of three dotted quarter notes each, making this a triple. And since each beat is made up of three notes, the meter is compound. Any time signature with a nine on top is a Compound Triple, including 9/2, 9/4, and 9/16.

Compound Quadruple. The time signature 12/8 is an example of a Compound Quadruple. There are four beats making it a quadruple, and three nots per beat making it a compound meter. Any meter with 12 on top is a Compound Quadruple, e.g., 12/8 and 12/16.

Composite Time

Time signatures with larger beat numbers are also possible, and these are known as composite meters. In such cases, the larger beat count is usually broken down into a combination of duples, triples or quadruples. In fact, any time the top number (beats per measure) is not divisible by 2 or 3, such as in time signatures like 5/4, 7/4 or 7/8, this is composite time.

For example, 5/4 meter most often has a 'one - two - three - one - two' or Strong, weak, weak, strong, weak feel, in effect acting as alternating bars of 3/4 + 2/4. This does not have to be the case though. Depending on the music, and the inclinations of the composer, the 5/4 meter could also be given a 2/4 + 3/4 tendency. For higher beat counts, many different breakdowns like this are technically possible. And while a composite time signature itself does not specifically indicate how the beat count should be split, there are some conventions for how it can be done. Two examples from popular music include Jethro Tull's "Living in the Past" (5/4 time) and Pink Floyd's "Money" (7/4 time).

Figure 7.8. Time Signatures of Popular Songs

2/2

"Paperback Writer" by The Beatles

"Blowin In The Wind" by Bob Dylan

"Your Time is Gonna Come" by Led Zeppelin

2/4

"Man of Constant Sorrow" from the movie O Brother Where Art Thou

3/4

"Piano Man" by Billy Joel

"Sweet Baby James" by James Taylor

"Scarborough Fair" by Simon & Garfunkel

4/4

"Smoke On The Water" by Jethro Tull

"Sweet Child o'Mine" by Guns N' Roses

"Beat It" by Michael Jackson

"Can't Help Falling In Love" by Elvis Presley

"Stand By Me" by Ben E. King

"You Can't Always Get What You Want" by The Rolling Stones

"These Boots Are Made For Walkin'" by Nancy Sinatra

"Space Oddity" by David Bowie

"The Sound Of Silence" by Simon & Garfunkel

6/8

"House of The Rising Sun" by Eric Burdon and The Animals

"We Are the Champions" by Queen

"Nothing Else Matters" by Metallica

12/8

"Whippin Post" by The Allman Brothers

"Norwegian Wood" by The Beatles

"Hallelujah" by Leonard Cohen

Another important piece of information communicated, at least indirectly, by a time signature is which beats are more important and should get accented.

Duple, triple, and quadruple meters have a characteristic beat emphasis hierarchy. In all three types, typically the first beat of every is the strongest and most important beat, and carries the most emphasis. So in duple time, the second beat is always weak and any subdivisions of the beat are weaker still. In quadruple time, however, beat three of the measure is actually stronger than beat two, but not quite as strong as beat one, and beat four is stronger still, and should lead into the next downbeat (beat one of the next measure). This arrangement of relative strength/weakness of beats is called the beat hierarchy. In contrast, Triple time starts with a strong beat one, has a weak beat two, and then begins to build on beat three with a beat stronger than two but weaker than one (leading to beat one again).

Finally, it is also important to realize that the Time Signature is also an indirect indicator of tempo. Music with a in 4/1 signature would likely move at a slower tempo than music with a 4/4 signature.

Polyrhythm

When the meter of a piece of music changes at some point in the music, this is called polyrhythm. A new time signature is usually placed at the start of each measure where a change occurs.

One such example is "We Can Work It Out" by The Beatles. The song is mostly in 4/4 until the bridge where it briefly goes into 3/4 for 4 bars. Another famous song for tricky time signatures is "Here Comes the Sun," as well as "Strawberry Fields Forever."

But there are times when the beats don't work out to be so nice and neat to fit with lyrics – and that's where a measure is thrown in with a different count to it, e.g. , 2/2, but the prevailing Time Signature is not changed. This can be found in Belinda Carlisle's "Heaven is a Place on Earth," The Beatles' "I Want You," Johnny Cash's "Ring of Fire," and Joan Jett's "I Love Rock n' Roll."

Expression

Musical expression is the art of playing or singing music with creative, original, clever, and pleasant sounding variations.

Being able to "feel" —sense, recognize, and comprehend—the rhythm of a piece of music, and then replicate it, is fundamental to being an effective musician. However, even when a musician knows the rhythm intended by a composer, playing the music following only that pattern is not always necessary or good. In fact, one of the most important creative elements in playing music is devising and making variations on, rhythms. For example, a musician might play a recognizable tune, but with a slightly altered rhythm, thus creating a new and slightly different experience of that tune. The listener's ear can still pick up the basic rhythm, but the variations (if not too large) add a pleasing 'fuzziness' to the timing of the music that actually enhances it. Think of Jimi Hendrix playing The Star Spangled Banner on his electric guitar.

Even within the performance of a particular song, variations on a beat pattern can be beneficial. For listeners, once a strong beat pattern has been established by a musician, it is often not necessary for the same things, or even anything, to happen on every beat, because the pattern has been recognized so it is expected to continue. When it doesn't, and the listener's expectations are not met, that can actually generate surprise and enhanced interest in the music.

In contrast, with computer music, where beats, notes, rests, etc., have been entered "precisely" via editing rather than being played by real musicians with real instruments, and creativity, the music often sounds quite rigid, mechanical and expressionless.

Chapter 8: Harmony and Chords

"Music, to create harmony, must investigate discord."
Plutarch

In music, when two or more notes are played simultaneously, whether the same note on different instruments, different notes on the same instrument, or different notes on different instruments, that is harmony. When we hear the playful blend of the voices in a barbershop quartet, or the majestic brilliance of a symphony orchestra with multiple sections of instruments playing at the same time, or the soothing and intricate blend of human voices in an a cappella choir, we get a true sense of the beauty of harmony in music. The richness of the sound generated by the unison of the different instruments or voices — a sound that none of them could have created individually—is the essence harmony.

Of course, music does not require harmony. You can have music that is just rhythm, e.g., drum solos, with no notes played at all and so no harmony. Similarly, you can have music that plays notes but never simultaneously, and so never creates harmony. Nevertheless, music theorists consider harmony to be one of the key elements of music, along with rhythm and melody.

Moreover, the word harmony can also be a bit misleading. When notes are being played simultaneously, they do not have to be particularly "harmonious" or consonant; they may instead be quite dissonant. So, the important fact for defining harmony is that the notes are sounding at the same time.

Chords

Harmonies with three or more notes are called chords and chords are derived from scales. In fact, each scale contains multiple possible chords, and it is usually quite easy to identify chords that are contained in any scale.

Chords, like scales, are also characterized by a set of intervals relative to the root note. For instance, a Major chord, which is derived from the Major scale, is a chord containing three notes. It is defined by the root and another note a major third above the root, and then another note a major third above the second note (and a perfect fifth above the root).

The way the notes in the chord relate back to its root note — is called the "spelling" of that chord, and this spelling is independent of the actual root note. So, if you know the name of the chord then you can easily determine the notes that are contained in it, regardless of what root note is used as the starting point. This spelling is often expressed as a series of numbers, e.g., 1 3 5, which actually corresponds to the degree numbers for the intervals in the scale from which the chord is derived.

As is the case with scales, degree numbers designate the intervals in a chord and how those intervals are arranged regardless of the root note. They do not correspond directly to notes until a root note is chosen, and the chord spelling then defines the chord.

For example, a "1 3 5 7" chord spelling, which is the formula for a Major 7th chord (more on this later) simply means that this chord consists of the Root (first scale degree), and the 3rd, 5th and 7th scale degree. If we take a Major scale, and assign it a key, let's say key of C, we can then simply apply this formula to determine the actual notes of the C Major 7th chord.

Also, because of variations in enharmonic spelling, it is important to remember that the same note can have differently names in different chords. For example, the chord B Major contains the note D#, taken from the B Major scale, while the same note is called E♭ when it appears in the A♭ Major chord, derived from the A♭ Major scale.

The notes of the chord are usually played at the same time (stacked chords) and this can be done on one polyphonic instrument, such as a piano or guitar, or they may be played simultaneously on multiple instruments, e.g., three woodwind instruments. However, they may also be played separately with some overlap, or played separately, but in a quick enough succession, that they will be "heard" as a chord (arpeggios). Moreover, some of the notes may be left out completely and only "implied" by the other two notes of the chord.

For example, instruments like the flute, trumpet, and obviously a single human voice, can sound only one note at once. Thus, they are monophonic instruments. Clearly then, these instruments cannot play a stacked chord where the notes are sounded simultaneously. Nevertheless, chords can still be implied. For example, since it is difficult to play three strings simultaneously on a violin (a not totally monophonic instrument), the two lower notes of the chord (sonority) are played in such a way that they resonate for a longer period of time, and the third note is then played with that resonance as the background sound, thus simulating the harmony of the chord. This technique is called a broken chord.

Also, the third note may not be played at all and instead just implied by the playing of the other two notes. Nevertheless, the listener "hears" a three-note harmonic structure. For example, in the key of C Major, if the music comes to rest on the two notes G and B, most listeners will hear this as a G major chord even when the third note is not sounded at all.

Finally, harmonization in chords usually sounds pleasant to the ear when there is a balance between the consonant and dissonant sounds. In simple words, that occurs when there is a balance between "tense" and "relaxed" moments (more on that later).

Chord Names

Since chords are derived from scales, the naming and notation conventions for chords are similar to those for scales. More specifically, different chords can be named by their "root note", e.g. C♯, and their characteristic "quality." For example, the chord Cmaj (or simply C) is a chord of the quality Major built on the root note C.

Minor chords are typically identified by a lowercase min, whereas chord quality is usually omitted for major chords. Similarly, + or aug is used for augmented chords, ° or dim (not -) for diminished chords, ø for half diminished chords, and dom for dominant chords. Additional symbols may also be added to the chord name to indicate if the chord is a triad, or some type of extended chord, e.g., a seventh (Δ7). Finally, any altered notes will also be identified (e.g. sharp five, or ♯5), as well as any added tones (e.g. add2) and the bass note if it is not the root (e.g. a slash chord).

For instance, for the chord name "C augmented seventh," the corresponding symbols could be Caug7, or C+7. Both are composed of three parts: 1 (letter 'C'), 2 ('aug' or '+'), and 3 (digit '7'). The three parts of the symbol (C, aug, and 7) refer to the root note C, the augmented (fifth) interval from C to G♯, and the (minor) seventh interval from C to B♭, respectively. These would then imply a chord formed by the notes C–E–G♯–B♭.

Types of Chords

<u>Triads</u>. Triads are the most commonly used type of chords and form the basis for most harmony in modern music. They are called triads called because they consist of three distinct notes, built from intervals of thirds, and with three relevant intervals total. In other words, they consist of a root note and two other notes above that root that ascend in thirds. So, starting with the root note, count up by a third (which means up two degrees in the scale) to get the next chord note, and then count up by another third to get the final chord note. And of course, don't forget that there is also an interval between the root and the top note, which is a perfect fifth.

The second note of a triad is called "the third" because it is an interval of a third away from the root of the chord. The "third" is especially important in constructing chords, as it is the quality of the "third" that determines whether you're dealing with a major or minor chord. A chord is called a minor triad if there's a minor third interval between the root and the third. A chord is called a major triad if there's a major third interval between the root and the third.

Also, the third and last note of a triad is of course called "the fifth," because it is a fifth interval from the root.

In fact, the most common triad chords are the Major and minor triads. But there are also augmented, diminished, and dominant triads.

A Major chord, as noted earlier, is made up of a root, a major third above the root, and a perfect fifth above the root. One way to see this is to start at the root, move up 4 half steps to the next note, then 3 half steps (or 7 total half steps above root) for the final note. The spelling of this chord is therefore "1 3 5." And, as mentioned before, the pattern is the same no matter the root note.

In contrast, a minor chord is made up of a root, a minor (or flattened) third above the root, and then a perfect fifth. In other words, starting at the root, go up 3 half steps to find the next note, and then another 4 half steps (7 half steps total above root). The spelling would thus be "min 1 3 5.

In an augmented triad chord, one note is actually raised a half step (sharpened) above where it is normally. So the formula you want to remember for building an augmented chord is: "1, 3, sharp 5." For example, for a Major chord, just take the first major scale degree, then the third major scale degree, and then the fifth major scale degree but raised by a half step.

It's also important to note here that "sharp 5" does not necessarily mean that the note will be a sharp, but rather that the "fifth" note will be raised, or sharpened, by a half step. Depending on the root you begin with, the result may in fact be a natural note.

A diminished triad chord consists of a root note, a minor third, and a diminished/flattened fifth. In a sense then, diminished triads are minor chords that have had both of the intervals between the third and fifth lowered by a half step. That means: first major scale degree, third major scale degree lowered one half step, and fifth major scale degree lowered one half step. Thus, the formula for building a diminished triad chords is: 1, flat 3, flat 5

Again, it's important to note here that flat 3 and flat 5 do not mean that these notes will necessarily be flats, but are only the third and fifth notes occurring in the scale degree lowered by a half step.

Another way of looking at a diminished triad is as a stack of minor intervals, with three half steps between each interval. So, for example, to build a C diminished triad (written as Cdim), you could build it by counting out the half steps between intervals, like this: Root position + 3 half steps + 3 half steps (6 half steps above root).

Diminished chords are not common, because they have a distinctive timbre: tense, dark, and unstable. However, one common use for the diminished chord is as a transition point between two other chords in a chord progression (more about this later). The diminished chord contains a high amount of tension, which is then can be released once the progression arrives on its finishing chord. Moreover, with the diminished chord as a transition, this also creates a stepwise motion in the root notes of the chords in the progression—they move up in half-step increments —which adds a powerful sense of movement to the music.

For example, in George Harrison's classic, "My Sweet Lord", the song starts on the key of E Major, and so the tonic chord is E maj, but there is also a brief alternation with C# min. Then this gives way to an F dim (diminished) chord, which serves as as transition that then gradually works its way to an F# min chord which becomes the finishing and resolving chord.

In summary, the major triad is very consonant; the minor triad is a bit less consonant but still enough so for most purposes. On the other hand, the augmented triad is very dissonant, and the diminished triad is extremely dissonant.

Figure 8.1. Common Triads

Type	Component Intervals		Chord Symbols	Notes
	Third	Fifth		
Major Triad	major	Perfect	C, CM, Cmaj, C∆, Cma	C E G
Minor Triad	minor	Perfect	Cm, Cmin, C−, Cmi	C E♭ G
Augmented Triad	major	Augmented	Caug, C$^+$, C+	C E G#
Diminished Triad	minor	Diminished	Cdim, C°, Cm$^{(♭5)}$	C E♭ G♭

Quadads. In many types of music, particularly contemporary instrumental and jazz, chords are often augmented with "tension". The tension is created by adding an additional note to the top of a triad chord that creates a relatively dissonant interval in relation to the root. Typically, this dissonant chord then "resolves" to a more consonant chord. When triads are augmented in this way, the result is usually obtained by adding a 7th of some kind (e.g., 1 3 5 7). That's why they're also often called 7th chords.

One of the most common 7th chords is the Major 7th. These chords have a major 3rd interval, followed by a minor 3rd, which is then followed by another major 3rd on top. This means that they have a Root, a Major 3rd, a Perfect 5th and a Major 7th and so the chord formula is: 1 3 5 7. In C, for example, the notes of C Major7 chord, or just CMaj7, or even CM7, would be: C E G B.

In contrast, a minor 7th chord is composed of a minor 3rd, followed by a major 3rd, followed by another minor 3rd. So, they have the following notes: Root, minor 3rd, Perfect 5th and a minor 7th. The chord formula is then: 1 flat3 5 flat7. So, in C, for example, the notes of the C minor 7, or Cm7, would be: C Eb G Bb.

Another common type of quadad is called the Dominant 7th. They have a Root, a Major 3rd, a Perfect 5th and then a minor 7th. So, a major 3rd interval is followed by two minor 3rd intervals. Thus, these chords are positioned somewhat in the middle between the Maj7 and min7 chords. However, the sound is quite different, with clear tension that is best resolved as part of a chord progression. The Chord formula for a dominant 7 is: 1 3 5 b7. For the C dominant 7, or just C7 (as it's usually written), the notes are then: C E G Bb.

The Minor 7 flat 5 chord just a minor 7th chord with a flattened 5th. It is composed of a: Root, a minor 3rd, a diminished 5th (a Tritone), and a minor 7th. This means that they have a minor 3rd interval followed by another minor 3rd, which is followed by a major 3rd (the opposite of Dominant 7). These very unique sounding chords are commonly used in jazz, sometimes in blues. The chord formula then is: 1 b3 b5 b7. So, for C minor 7b5, or Cm7b5, the notes would be: C Eb Gb Bb.

The Diminished 7 or Full Diminished chord is composed of stacked minor 3rd intervals, which is why they are also often called symmetrical chords. Any chords that have the same intervals across all their notes are symmetrical. Their interval structure is always the same, no matter if you're ascending or descending in pitch. In practice, this means that you can move these chords up or down by a minor 3rd interval (3 semitones) as much as you want, and the notes would remain the same, only in different order. The sound of diminished 7 chord can be described as jarring, dark and unstable, but also interesting and is often used in music to add a dramatic effect.

Diminished 7 chords should not be mistaken with diminished triads, which are typically just called 'diminished' chords. Specifically, diminished 7ths consist of a Root, minor 3rd, diminished 5th, and Major 6th. Chord formula is: 1 b3 b5 bb7. Of course, the bb7 simply means a double flatted 7th, which is in effect the same as the 6th scale degree. For example, for the C diminished 7, or Cdim7 for short, the notes are then: C Eb Gb Bbb.

These of course are not all of the possible combinations of intervals from which quadads can be constructed. There are quite a few more, e.g., Major and minor 6ths, or a Dominant 7 chord with a flat 5th (1 3 b5 b7), etc. But if you know what types of intervals you want to build the chord from, and then create the appropriate chord formula, and choose a root note, you can then quickly determine the chord notes. If course, the real test will be in then hearing the chord sounded out. At that point you will know better how the chord might best be used, if at all.

Figure 8.2. Common Quadads

Type	Component Intervals			Chord Symbols	Notes
	Third	Fifth	Seventh		
Diminished Seventh	minor	Diminished	Diminished	C°7, Cdim7	C E♭ G♭ B𝄫
Half Diminished Seventh	minor	Diminished	minor	Cø7, Cm7♭5, C−(♭5)	C E♭ G♭ B♭
Minor Seventh	minor	Perfect	minor	Cm7, Cmin7, C−7	C E♭ G B♭
Minor Major Seventh	Minor	Perfect	Major	CmM7, Cmmaj7, C−(j7), C−∆7, C−M7	C E♭ G B
Dominant Seventh	Major	Perfect	Minor	C7, Cdom7	C E G B♭
Major Seventh	Major	Perfect	Major	CM7, Cᴹ7, Cmaj7, C∆7, Cj7	C E G B
Augmented Seventh	Major	Augmented	Minor	C+7, Caug7, C7+, C7+5, C7♯5	C E G♯ B♭
Augmented Major Seventh	Major	Augmented	Major	C+M7, CM7+5, CM7♯5, C+j7, C+∆7	C E G♯ B

Open and Closed Voicing

When all the notes of a chord are in the same octave, the chord is considered to be in a closed voicing. However, sometimes the notes of a triad may be spread out over two or more octaves, or with the different notes rearranged so that, for example, the root may carry the highest sounding note, or the third, or the fifth can carry the lowest sounding note. The notes are still the same (C, E, G, for example) — they're just located an octave or even octaves above or below where you would expect them in a normal triad. This is called open voicing.

Inversion

Chords may also be inverted, changing the order in which the notes are stacked. If the third of a chord is the lowest-sounding note, then it is said that the chord is in "first inversion." When the fifth of a chord is the lowest-sounding note, the chord is in "second inversion." When a seventh of a chord is the lowest-sounding note, then that chord is in "third inversion."

Chord Notation

For the benefit of performers, chords can be represented in various ways on a musical staff. However, some of these methods are more commonly used than others. One common method is to simply represent the notes of the chord on the staff in their normal relative positions.

Figure 8.3. Chords on Musical Staff

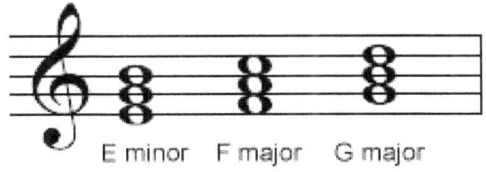

Another approach is to write the chord names (letter and quality) above the staff. This tells the performer what chord should be played until the next name appears. Chord names also may be used even when the chord notes are written out on the staff, so that performers can read either the chord names or the notated music, as they prefer.

Figure 8.4. Chords on Musical Staff With Chord Names Above

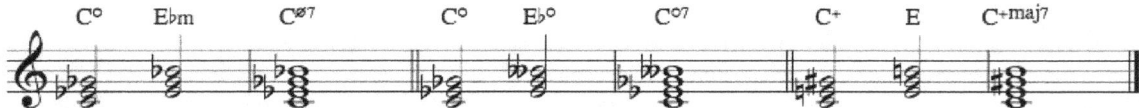

Chord Charts

In an effort to simplify things for musicians, various other approaches to notating relevant chords for a piece of music have been developed over the years and are commonly used. One of these is the chord chart.

A chord chart describes the basic harmonic and rhythmic information for a piece of music and is intended to quickly lay out a rough outline so that the musician may improvise around it. Consequently, it is most commonly used by professional session musicians playing jazz or popular music where improvisation is expected. The chord chart is usually intended for the rhythm section (e.g., piano, guitar, drums and bass) to provide them with the minimal amount of information necessary to create the acoustic and rhythmic foundation for the music. The other musicians are then expected to improvise the individual notes used for the chords (the "voicing") and the appropriate ornamentation, counter melody or bass line.

In some chord charts, the harmony is provided as a series of chord symbols above a traditional musical staff. The rhythmic information is usually written using a special form of "rhythmic notation" and it can be very specific.

Figure 8.5. A Chord Chart

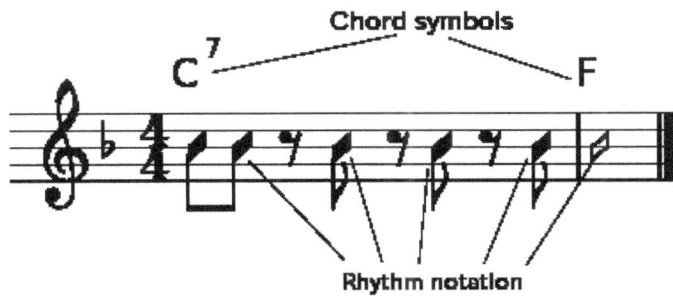

However, another approach is completely non-specific. This "slash notation" approach allows the musician to fill the measure with chords or any other way he or she sees fit (comping).

Figure 8.6. A Chord Chart With Slash Notation

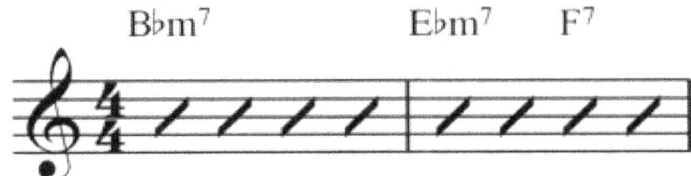

A similar simplifying technique is the lead sheet (or fake sheet) which specifies the essential elements of a popular song: the melody, the lyrics, and the harmony. The melody is written in modern Western music notation, the lyrics are written as text below the staff, and the harmony is specified with chord symbols above the staff. No chord voicing, voice leading, bass line or other aspects of the accompaniment are specified by the lead sheet. These are determined later by an arranger or improvised by performers. Sometimes, a lead sheet may also specify an instrumental part or theme, when this essential to the song's identity. For example, in Deep Purple's "Smoke on the Water", the opening guitar riff is a crucial identifying element of the song; any performance of the song should include the guitar riff, and any imitation of that guitar riff would be an illegal imitation of the song. Thus, the riff belongs on the lead sheet.

Finally, sometimes collections of lead sheets for various songs will be compiled and perhaps even published legally, or sometimes illegally without giving appropriate credit or paying required royalties to the composers or musicians. These are known as a fake book.

Chord Progressions

A chord progression or a harmonic progression is a series of chords played in a sequence. Chord progressions can provide not only the foundation of the harmony for a piece of music, but also form the basis for the melody and the rhythm of the music. They can also create a sense of 'movement' within the music. A chord progression usually "aims for a definite goal" of establishing (or contradicting) a tonality founded on a key, root, or tonic chord.

Although any chord may in principle be followed by any other chord, certain patterns of chord progressions have been accepted and are more commonly used because they clearly establish a root and key (tonic note) that then resolves the chord sequence to a tonic chord.

Musicians may describe a specific chord progression (for example, "two measures of G major, then a half measure of A minor and a half measure of D seventh", or just "G, A minor, D seventh") or speak more generally of classes of chord progressions (for example a "blues chord progression").

In fact, one frequently used chord progression in Western traditional music and blues is the 12-measure blues progression. It is a good one for you to learn. For example, in C Major, a simple 12-measure blues progression can be built using C, F and G major chords. Just allocate four beats to each chord symbol (48 beats total over 12 measures).

12-Bar Blues in C Major:

C-C-C-C

F-F-C-C

G-F-C-C

Chord progressions do not need to be long or complicated. One of the real talents of many composers is keeping the music simple, but still making it sound complex and fully developed.

Finally, it is important to note that Roman numerals are often used to indicate the chords in a progression. They identify the musical key and the root note for each chord. Uppercase Roman numerals represent major chords, while lowercase numerals represent minor chords. For example, a chord progression in the key of C major would look like I-vi-IV-V (C-Am-F-G).

Chapter 9: Melody and Dynamics

"Funny how a melody sounds like a memory."
Eric Church

While a note is a single sound with a particular pitch and duration, a melody is at the very least a sequence of several notes. Of course, it is usually much more than that. More specifically, a melody is a creatively arranged sequence of notes, with variations in pitch, duration, tempo, accent, articulation, and rhythm. In fact, it may be legitimately argued that melody is the single most important element of music. When we think of a piece music, we naturally think of the melody as well.

And while you may sometimes hear someone describe a piece of music as having "no melody," technically that is incorrect. The music may have a melody that is not particularly distinctive, clever, complex, well-developed, creative, or memorable, but it nonetheless has a melody. Of course, when a melody does have such qualities, it is more likely to get your attention, capture your ear, compel you to continue listening, impact you emotionally, and make the musical experience much more memorable.

Melody is a particularly difficult musical concept to describe or explain. The creative options for composing melodies are so numerous, varied, and flexible that entire books have been written on the topic of melody and still have not even come close to covering the topic completely. So, I will not attempt to do so here.

One thing that can be achieved, however, and which is the goal of this chapter, is to identify the typical components of a melody, discuss some important concepts related to how melodies vary, and explain some of the compositional options available to composers and provide some examples of how they might be used.

More specifically, music theorists discuss the characteristics of melodies in relation to concepts such as musical phrases, periods, cadence, motifs, themes, shape, contour, and motion.

Musical Phrases

As a starting point, any melody can be described as made up of musical phrases, which in many ways are like a phrases in verbal or written communication. A phrase in a sentence ("into the deep, cold ocean" or "underneath that car") is a group of words that make sense together and express a clear and definite idea. However, typically, a phrase is not a complete sentence. In a similar way, a musical phrase is a group of notes that fit together and creatively express a definite musical "idea" but often not a complete musical "sentence" (more on that later).

There is of course no set length for a musical phrase. It is not uncommon to find 16-measure or even 32-measure long phrases, especially in music with a very fast tempo. Some phrases can even be very short, as is common in exceptionally slow or rhythmically complex music. In language, this might be similar to short declarative sentences like "Stop!" or "Come here." Phrase lengths do tend to remain constant in a given piece (or section) of music, and the most common phrase length in music is actually around four measures.

Cadence.

Just as we typically pause between the different "phrases" in a sentence (for example, when I say, "whatever you do, don't go there"), a melody may pause slightly at the end of one musical phrase, before moving on to the next one. Also, like a period at the end of a sentence, a melody may also communicate or "punctuate" closure in some way at the end of a phrase. In fact, there may even be cues that signal to the listener that the end of a phrase is approaching.

In vocal music, the musical phrasing tends to follow closely with the phrases and pauses of the lyrics, especially when the singer needs to take a breath. But even without lyrics, the musical phrases in a melody can be very clearly defined as separate melodic "ideas". These pauses, cues, or punctuations at the end of a musical phrases are called cadence.

Composers use various methods to create a cadence or a sense of "finish" for each musical phrase. In fact, one way that a composer can make a piece of music more interesting is by varying how clearly the end of each phrase is made apparent. Some common methods include:

Harmony - One of the most important and most commonly used signals of cadence is harmony. For example, a piece of music may end on a tonic chord (a chord based on the tonic note for the scale from which the chord is derived). But a tonic chord by itself will not necessarily be perceived as an ending; an appropriate chord progression (at least two chords) must "lead up to" the tonic. This "voice leading" creates a sense of the inevitability for the tonic chord to be heard as an ending. Typically, smaller moves between harmonically related chords in a chord progression sound more natural and pleasing.

When harmony is used to establish cadence, it can be done in several ways.

Authentic Cadence. For authentic cadence, a simple two chord progression is used. The progression uses the dominant triad chord (a chord based on the fifth tone of the scale from which the chord is derived) which is then followed by the tonic triad (based on the tonic of the same scale). In standard Roman numeral notation, the chord progression would be V-I.

If the upper voice of the progression (treble clef) proceeds stepwise either upward from the leading tone (seventh degree of the scale from which the chord is derived) or downward from the second degree to the tonic note, while the lowest voice (bass clef) skips from the dominant note upward a fourth or downward a fifth to the tonic note, this is called perfect cadence. It is in fact the strongest and most effective form harmonic cadence.

Half Cadence (semi-cadence). Half cadence ends the phrase on a dominant chord (a chord based on the fifth tone of the scale from which the chord is derived), and so does not sound final. In other words, the phrase ends with unresolved harmonic tension. Thus, a half cadence typically signals to the listener that another phrase will follow, ending with an authentic cadence and finality (more on that later).

Deceptive Cadence (interrupted cadence). A deceptive cadence begins with the dominant chord (V), like an authentic cadence. However, it does not end on the tonic chord (I). Instead, the triad built on the sixth degree (VI, the submediant) substitutes for the tonic, with which it shares two of its three pitches. A deceptive cadence is often used to extend a phrase, to overlap one phrase with another, or to facilitate a sudden modulation to a different key.

Plagal Cadence. In plagal cadence, a subdominant chord (a chord based on the fourth note of the scale from which the chord is derived) is followed by a tonic chord (IV-I). This cadence is typically used to an extend an authentic cadence. The most common example of plagal cadence is the final "Ahhh—Men" (IV–I) at the end of hymns in Christian church services.

Rhythm and Tempo - Changes in the rhythm, a break or pause using a musical rest, extending the length of notes, slowing the tempo, or slurring a series of notes, can also be used to manifest cadence.

Melodic Articulation - Various notes or sequences of notes may be modified slightly in various ways in order to call attention to them. For example, the pitch, duration, timbre, intensity, or even how the notes start or end (more abruptly, more gradually) can all be altered slightly. Melodic articulation is similar to articulation in speech and tactics by which the attention and interest of the listener can be maintained through different creative ways of phrasing common ideas. Such modifications, then, can also be used to establish cadence in a melody.

However it is achieved, the most important characteristic of any cadence is its perceived degree of finality. The stronger the sense of finality, the greater the conviction of conclusiveness, and the more clear the "finished" quality exhibited by a cadence, the stronger the cadence.

Antecedent and Consequent Phrasing

Often phrases come in definite pairs, with the first phrase feeling very unfinished, open, or weak (half cadence) until it is completed by the second phrase that feels stronger, more complete, or closed (authentic or perfect cadence). In fact, for the listener it may often sound as if the second phrase were responding to a call or answering a question from the first phrase. When phrases come in pairs like this, the first phrase is called the antecedent phrase, and the second is called the consequent phrase. The composer's ability to evoke such feelings of expectation and then fulfillment will contribute significantly to the listener's enjoyment of the music.

Together, the pair of phrases is a "period" (think of it as like complete sentence). The typical period is then eight measures long containing two four-measure phrases.

For example, consider the nursery rhyme, Mary Had a Little Lamb.

When you get to the end of the first line, 'Mary had a little lamb, little lamb, little lamb,' there's a natural pause. This is the end of the first musical phrase of this song and is also the antecedent phrase. And notice how, in this case, simple repetition of one element of the phrase is used to set up this pause as a weak cadence. However, we would certainly never end the song here. In fact, the weak cadence at the end of the first phrase sets us up to "expect" something to come after it to complete it; it feels unfinished.

Then, the second line of the song completes or "finishes" the "sentence" for us: 'Mary had a little lamb; its fleece was white as snow.'

Notice how the entire musical thought sounds and how it now feels finished. We could easily end the song here because it feels good; it feels complete. This second line is also a musical phrase, but in contrast to the first phrase, it is the consequent phrase and it ends with a strong cadence—hence, the feeling of completeness. The result, then, is:

'Mary had a little lamb, little lamb, little lamb. Mary had a little lamb; its fleece was white as snow.'

In addition to having an antecedent-consequent relationship to each other, two phrases contained in a period may also differ in their degree of similarity to each other. For example, sometimes the second phrase will be identical (or parallel) to the first one, except for the cadence; or the second phrase may be similar to the first one but vary slightly in pitches, durations, tempo, etc.; or the phrases may truly be contrasting or completely different, while still maintaining their relative cadence relationship.

Moreover, while most periods consist of a pair of phrases, it is possible for them to have three (or more) phrases, some of which may be repetitions of each other. Also, two periods can even be grouped into what is called a double-period.

Other Phrase Transitions (bridges)
Of course, melodies don't always divide into clearly separated phrases or periods. Often the phrases in a melody will run into each other, cut each other short, or overlap. In

fact, the goal of a composer is to keep the music interesting and moving forward, and create a sense of continuation for the listener. Hence, the spaces between phrases demand special attention. Special care must be taken to not to let the music "sag" or come to a complete stop prematurely. There are many different techniques for managing these transition points.

For example, phrase elision is a special device for joining phrases together in an overlapping manner. In elision, the final bar of one phrase is simultaneously the first bar of the next phrase.

Other transition techniques include: lead-ins, in which a special short measure of music serves to transition between phrases; extension or expansion, when some additional material is appended to the end of a phrase to delay its cadence, or the entire phrase, part of the phrase, or the phrase cadence is repeated, often with some variation or embellishment, prolonging the closure of the phrase; or truncations, where the standard phrase can have a piece "missing", measures that seemingly should be present but are not, shortening the phrase.

Motif and Themes

Some phrases have detectable divisions made of two or more smaller parts. These smaller segments are called motifs (motives).

A motif is a short musical idea - shorter than a phrase. It may also be called a cell or a figure, and it is in fact the smallest structural unit in music that communicates a musical thought or idea. These small pieces of melody will typically be repeated many times in a piece of music, often exactly the same as before. However, when repeated, the motif may also be embellished or differently articulated in some way: it may be played slower or faster; it may be played in a different key; it may played by a different instrument or sung in a different voice; it may be reversed; it may start on a different note; it may be inverted with the notes going up instead of down; it may be played with larger or smaller intervals between the notes; it may be repeated one or more times in sequence with slight variations; it may have notes removed or added; or the pitches or rhythms may be altered in some other way.

Most motifs are shorter than phrases, but sometimes they can be long enough to also be considered phrases. For example, in background music for TV shows or movies (e.g., Star Wars), musicals (e.g., West Side Story), and operas (e.g., those by Wagner), there are "leitmotifs" which are short musical phrases associated with a particular character, place, thing, or idea. It will typically be heard whenever that character comes on stage or the screen, or the scene moves back to a particular place. And, as with other motifs, leitmotifs may be altered slightly when played again. For example, the same motif may sound quite different depending on whether the character associated with it is in love and happy, fighting, or dying.

A longer section of melody that keeps reappearing in the music is often called a theme. Themes generally are at least one phrase long and often have several phrases. Many longer works of music, such as symphony movements, have more than one melodic theme.

Musical scores for movies and television can also contain melodic themes, which can be developed as they might be in a symphony or may be used very much like operatic leitmotifs.

For example, in the music John Williams composed for the Star Wars movies, there are melodic themes that are associated with the main characters. These themes are often complete melodies with many phrases, but a single phrase can be taken from the melody and used as a motif. A single phrase of Ben Kenobi's Theme, for example, can remind you of all the good things he stands for, even if he is not on the movie screen at the time.

Melodic Shape, Contour, and Motion

A melody that stays on the same pitch gets boring pretty quickly. Consequently, as a melody progresses, the pitches typically change, getting higher or lower according to some pattern and/or slowly or quickly. In fact, much of a melody's expressiveness is based on the upward or downward flow of pitch. More specifically, when the pitch of a song goes up, it can make the song sound like it's getting more tense or more lively. In contrast, if the pitch of a song goes down, it can give that part of the song an increased melancholic or dark feel. The shape of the pitches travel is called its contour.

Moreover, when a melody rises and falls, and does so slowly, with only small pitch changes between one note and the next, it is a conjunct melody. One may also speak of such a melody in terms of step-wise or scalar motion, since most of the intervals in the melody are half (minor second) or whole steps (major second) or are part of a scale (steps). However, when a melody rises and falls quickly, with large (minor third or larger) intervals between one note and the next (skips or leaps), it is a disjunct melody. Many great melodies are a mixture of conjunct and disjunct motion.

There are four common melodic contours: Arch, Wave, Inverted Arch, and Pivotal

Arch - The melody first goes up in pitch from a low point to a high point, then goes back down again. When music goes up in pitch gradually like this, it results in an increase in tension in that section of the composition. The lower the pitch gets in such a gradual arch, the more the level of tension decreases.

Wave - The melody line goes up, and down, and up again, and down — just like a series of waves. The wave contour permeates most happy-sounding pop music.

Inverted Arch - In the inverted arch contour, the pitch starts out high, goes down, and then up again. The phrase will therefore start out sounding relaxed and calm, but contain an increase in tension as the arch rises towards the end of the phrase.

Pivotal - The pivotal contour revolves around a certain pitch (e.g. E). It's a lot like a wave melody, except that the movement above and below the central note is minimal and continuously returns to that central note. Traditional folk music uses the pivotal melodic pattern a lot.

Any melody line in a piece of music will generally fall into one of these categories of contour.

Counterpoint

When more than one melody is being played simultaneously, or at least in ways that overlap, the music is contrapuntal, and the melodic lines are called counterpoint, especially for piano music or multi-instrumental music. In contrast, vocal music with one or more harmonic parts being sung simultaneously or nearly simultaneously, may be described as polyphony or polyphonic music, but it would only be contrapuntal if the different choral parts are truly different melodies independent of each other.

In many traditional choral pieces, there are four very different singing parts (soprano, alto, tenor, and bass), and each part, sung alone, can seem like its own melody. But the parts have basically the same rhythms, so that the effect, when sung together, is of harmonic chords (homophonic) being sung by one voice. Barbershop quartet music is another good example of vocal homophonic, or chordal, music, which is not considered contrapuntal.

In any event, contrapuntal refers to two or more simultaneous and independent melodies. "Simultaneous" means the melodies are happening at the same time. "Independent" means that at any given moment what is happening in one melody (both in the rhythms and in the pitches) is probably not the same thing that is happening in the other melody. What is most important is that these melodies work together to create pleasant sounding music overall.

Obviously, there is no counterpoint if there is no melody at all. Similarly, if there is one melodic line accompanied only by rhythm, or a background drone, or only by chords, there is no counterpoint. Even when different people are singing or playing different parts, it is not necessarily considered counterpoint if the parts are not independent enough, or if one of the parts is very clearly a dominating melody.

One of the simplest and most familiar types of counterpoint is the round (e.g., Row, Row, Row Your Boat). In a round, everyone sings the same melody, but they start singing it at different times. Although everyone is singing exactly the same tune, at any particular time different people will be singing different parts of it, so the final effect is of independent parts.

In a dixieland band, the instruments that are playing the melody are also generally playing independent parts, giving the music a complex or "busy" sound. In fact, when music sounds very "busy" or when there is so much going on that it gets difficult to decide where the melody is or what part to sing along with, it is likely that you are hearing counterpoint.

Dynamics

Melodies are not just a series of notes rising or falling in pitch. Music is a language, and a piece of music is a story. And like any good story, there should be change, development, expression, climaxes, and periods of tension and periods of release. In fact, it is through variations in the dynamic qualities of music that composers and performers convey emotion in music or create drama.

In a previous chapter, I discussed how composers may want specific variations in tempo and rhythm to occur at various points in a piece of music, and how they communicate this using dynamic markings. However, tempo or rhythm variations are not the only ones possible. The volume, intensity, style, and articulation of the music may also be creatively varied in certain places.

<u>Volume and Intensity</u> - Sometimes, composers want a certain set of notes, a musical phrase, or a larger section of the music played louder or quieter, or more intensely, as a way of making the music more attention getting or interesting. When discussing the

physics of sound earlier, I noted that variations of intensity or volume may be measured by physicists and audio engineers in decibels. However, in music notation, variations in volume or intensity are not treated as absolute values, but rather as relative ones.

As was the case with tempo, composers use special dynamic markings to communicate that the music is to become louder or quieter, and these markings can be placed at the beginning or anywhere else within a piece of music.

There are basically two different ways of notating volume and intensity dynamics.

One approach indicates a single, unchanging level of volume until another dynamic marking appears to change it. This begins with the Italian words like "forte" (f) for loud and "piano" (p) for soft. These can then be modified by adding additional words in order to provide more specific guidance. For example, "mezzo piano" (mp) for moderately soft and "mezzo forte" (mf) for moderately loud are common notations. Similarly, "fortepiano" (fp) may be used to communicate a loud beginning or "attack" with a sudden decrease to a soft level. The full span of these markings range from pianissississimo (pppp) for nearly inaudible to fortissississimo (ffff) which means "as loud as possible."

However, because such dynamic markings are subject to individual interpretation, another somewhat more informative approach was developed. Graded dynamic markings are used to indicate a progressive increase in loudness or softness, respectively, based on the Italian words crescendo (getting louder) or decrescendo (getting quieter). On a page of music, these markings often look like a hairpin, either expanding to the right for a crescendo or gradually contracting to the right for a decrescendo.

<u>Style</u> - In addition to changes in tempo or volume, dynamic markings are also frequently used to specify alterations in the style or mood with which the music is performed by various instruments. These are also typically indicated by verbal instructions written at various points on the musical staff. For example, the word "dolce" (sweetly), usually written above the staff over the measures to which it pertains, indicates a soft and "sweet" timbre. Similarly, "sul tasto" instructs a string player to move their bow near or

over the fingerboard to produce a less brilliant sound. "Cuivre" instructs a brass player to produce a forced and stridently brassy sound.

Other common style instructions include:

Agitato: Excitedly, agitated

Animato: With spirit

Appassionato: Impassioned

Con forza: Forcefully, with strength

Dolce: Sweetly

Dolente: Sadly, with great sorrow

Grandioso: Grandly

Legato: Smoothly, with the notes flowing from one to the next

Sotto voce: Barely audible

<u>Articulation</u> - Articulation is the technique with which the performer plays the notes. For example, "staccato" is the intentional shortening of note duration compared to the written note value, thus giving a quickened popping quality to the sound. On the other hand, "legato" instructs that the notes be played in a smoothly joined sequence with no separation. In fact, one common dynamic marking is the slur. Just like when your speech is slurred and the words strung together into a continuous sound, a musical slur is to be played with all the notes "slurring" into one another. On a musical scale, are indicated by curved lines that tie the notes together.

Other common articulation marks.

legato (smooth, connected);

tenuto (pressed or played to full notated duration);

marcato (accented and detached);

staccato ("separated", "detached");

martelé (heavily accented or "hammered");

staccatissimo (even more sharply separated than staccato);

Many of these can be combined to create certain "in-between" articulations. For example, portato is the combination of tenuto and staccato. Also, some instruments have unique methods by which to produce sounds, such as spiccato for bowed strings, where the bow is bounced off the string.

Of course, like any other dynamic markings, articulation marks are imprecise and so open to interpretation or subject to the personal whims and style of a given musician. The manner in which a performer decides to execute a given articulation is usually based on the context of the piece or phrase, may also depend on the instrument (e.g., strings, wind, etc.) and the genre of the music (Classical, Baroque, Jazz, etc.).

Chapter 10: Final Thoughts

"I don't sing because I'm happy; I'm happy because I sing."
William James

Music is inextricably woven into human existence. Just as is the case with language, music is fundamentally a part of who we are as human beings, how we think, how we feel, and how we communicate with each other. It also, in many ways, defines who we are as members of any particular culture, generation, or society. In other words, understanding music means understanding ourselves.

The purpose of this book is to serve as an introduction to what music is and how it is done. The hope is that such a foundation in the basics of music theory will be useful to musicians, composers, lyricists, music critics, educators, and music therapists, as well as provide a common language with which members of these music related professions might more effectively communicate with each other.

For musicians, and composers in particular, the hope is that this book may also provide a better sense of the full range of their performance and compositional options — more specifically with regard to relevance of and use of intervals, scales, keys, tempo, meter, rhythm, harmony, chords and chord progressions, and the construction of distinctive musical phrases and more dynamic and memorable melodies. In other words, to help them make better music.

Of course, composers typically do not compose with some type of checklist of options or a glossary of terminology next to them, and I am not suggesting that they do. There was a time at the beginning of the 20th century when composers tried formulaic writing, but most of the 12-tone row compositions were not welcomed by the general audience. If you want to hear some, check out Webern 'Sehr Langsam' or Stravinsky 'The

Rite of Spring'. Composers may instead, based on experience alone, know intuitively what sounds good and what does not, and so purely by accident may include creative and distinctive motifs in their music, for example, without even knowing that what they have included is called a motif, or really even care. For music theorists, that is not a problem at all. Nothing is this book is intended to be limiting or prescriptive in any way, but rather simply informative and guiding.

Essential to all music, after all, is choice, imagination, inspiration, originality, creativity, cleverness, expression, distinctiveness, innovation, and style.